Mortgage Loan Processing Training

Easy step-by-step Guide

Your Guide to Success

BarginHouse Publications © 2008
Printed in the USA

**Mortgage Loan Processing Training Manual
Step-by-Step Guide**

http://www.loanprocessors101.com/
www.trainingloanofficer.com

Barginhouse Publications
www.locareertraining.com

Chicago, IL.

ISBN# 978-1-4357-1118-1
Library of Congress Control Number: 2008910364

Copyright © 2008

All rights reserved..
No part of this publication may be reproduced or stored reproduced in any form or by any means, electronic, mechanical, photocopying, recording, or other wise, without the written permission of the publisher.

Printed in the United States of America

Preface

**Considering a Career as a Mortgage Loan Processor?
Congratulations! You Can Do It!**

Becoming a mortgage loan processor is probably one of the wisest career decisions you have ever made. It's an ideal way for an average person to enter into a high paying market with growth potential. Although the economy goes up and down like a roller coaster, one thing for certain, everyone, everywhere will continue to purchase and sell homes, refinance their existing home or business, land or investments on a daily basis. Consider the cost of our health insurance, gas prices and the cost of food, prices rise and fall constantly but the peoples continue to indulge in these things. We continue to eat, drive and purchase homes all over the globe, some owning several, so therefore these things are necessities and are in demanded daily. It seems as the media only reports the crisis… Think back to the hurricanes, have you ever heard so much coverage? Reporting bad news keep them employed, good news doesn't sell or is boring to the general public.

Getting your foot in the door will open up a number of opportunities. You may later decide to become a Loan Originator, a broker or a Realtor? Successful loan processors and Loan Officers are no different than you; they simply apply the principles and techniques taught here. These techniques have been proven to make others successful in the past. Your success will depend on your own goals and efforts. There is absolutely no limit to your potential. Opportunity is knocking **NOW**, but you must take the first step and keep walking!

Just please keep in mind that this is not a get rich quick program.

Being successful in any area of our life takes dedication, training and striving toward achieving your goals, "this applies to everything in life!"

One very important quality every individual should possess in this Industry or any other field of work is confidence. If you lack confidence in yourself you will not successfully be able to convince an employer to entrust his business into your hands, nor will you trust your own ability. You must believe in yourself in order to succeed in life. Anyone can learn anything if they apply themselves wholeheartedly to whatever they desire.

The information in this Training Manual/Study Guide has been compiled and written by a group of experienced Mortgage Loan Officers, Loan Processors and other professionals in the Mortgage field for the sole purpose of training new mortgage loan processors.
This training manual focuses on the practical aspects of residential mortgage lending and is believed to be accurate at the time of publishing.

This Publication is designed to provide accurate and authoritative information in regards to the subject matter covered. It is solid with understanding that the publisher is not engaged in rendering legal accounting or other professional services. If legal advise or other expert assistance is required, the services of a competent professional person should be sought.

Please Note* This Training Manual is your basic training and does not guarantee the same system and techniques to every company and state... We take no responsibility whatsoever for any information that does not apply to your state or company, nor are we responsible for changes in the system or laws that apply to Home Mortgages and the financial lending system. Laws, rules and changes are beyond our control, and we advise you seek updates and changes from your local state and federal government, such as Fannie Mae and Freddie Mac and other sources.

Contents

Helpful Hints

Introduction

Summary

4 Terms you should know

Getting Started

First Contacts

10 Basic Steps

Step 1 Inquire of the Loan Officer is this Purchase or Refinancing
Step 2 Inquire of the Loan Officer is this Full Documentation Loan or No Income Verification Loan
Step 3 Check, verify and enter loan application's information complete and accurate is vital
Step 4   Obtain copy of sales contract
Step 5   Copy of earnest check front and back
Step 6   Request borrower's W2'S, Recent Pay Stubs
Step 7   Obtain copies of 40 IK, IRA, Life Insurance (FACE VALUE)
Step 8   Home Owners Insurance Binder and PMI
Step 9   Order title and Appraisal
Step 10 Check all information + documents and submit completed package / file to Underwriting

Conditions
Quick Recap
Understanding Credit Report
Understanding the Loan Application
Request Forms
Understanding The Appraisal
Glossary

Acknowledgement

Although this manual is a step-by-step guide, it is impossible to teach anyone everything in one book. The author of this book cannot guarantee that all information in this training manual applies to every financial institution or lender as state-by-state and individual lenders vary by rules and laws. The author of this book cannot guarantee that all information in this manual is accurately up to date as rules and laws are often updated and changed. The author and publisher of this Training Manual recommend that you periodically check you're your local state and government for all changes and updates concerning the Mortgage lending and financial institution.

Our Mortgage Loan Processing manual will train you in all the basics as well as the ins and outs of the processing of mortgage loans. With some additional research and resources you will be greatly informed and well on the way to becoming a successful Mortgage Loan Processor earning a substantial income.

Congratulations, You can only grow from this point on but always remember this- Success is Earned, Not just learned.

Note: Some of our pages are intentionally left blank, blurred or distorted to protect real information. Clear copies of every document used in this manual is accessible on the internet and can be clearly viewed or printed off any computer with a printer. All these documents can be found via google search or by visiting Fannie Mae or Freddie Mac website.
This manual explains the steps of traditional mortgage loan processing. After completing this section you should have a basic understanding of mortgage loan processing as well as the mortgage terms so you will a better understand of the mortgage loan process.

Again Note: The author and publisher accept no responsibility or guarantee as to the accuracy of subject matter in this manual as it varies from state to state and can change at anytime.

The reader is advised to refer to the industry procedure manuals of FNMA (Fannie Mae) or FHLMC (Freddie Mac) for clarification.
Additional Forms, Applications and information can be downloaded free at

HUD RESPA - OCM Forms - Freddie Mac As well as many other sites

Helpful Hints
NOTES:

*Helpful Hint #1 ---Form an automatic system and create you a checklist

When processing a mortgage loan, it's a good idea to have some sort of checklist in each file. This will enable you to keep track of what documents you have and those that you need to receive.

Most lenders require you to put the documents in what is know as a stacking order.
The stacking order helps the loan officers and underwriters look through your file with ease. If the documents are grouped together in a certain order, the speed of your file being underwritten in a timely fashion is increased.
Some lenders have their own stacking order, but most will accept a file that's organized neatly by you.

During the mortgage process, most documents you receive will come via fax. It is very important that you make clean, eligible copies, with accurate information. Documents that can't be read will slow or delay the loan process.

It is always a good idea to have the original documents available when requested by the lender or underwriter that's going to close and fund the loan. Most processors send a copy of the file to the lender until they have gotten a clear to close, at which point you should be prepared to send the original file with original signatures to the lender.

Always remember to keep a copy of the file for your records.

Please Note: Some of our documents are intentionally blurred or have been blotted out for the purpose of hiding our address and other personal information because these documents are of actual properties. The documents that are blurred are documents that you should be familiar with and not actually require any work on your part.

Introduction

So, you want to be a Mortgage Loan Processor.

This manual was written with the intent of teaching an individual about mortgage loan processing by experienced loan processors who are associated with financial institutions and mortgage brokerage firms. The loan processor has a critical role in the mortgage loan transaction.

As a processor, you will have a great deal of interaction with the loan originator, underwriter, attorney's, appraisers and insurance companies. You will also be responsible for working with the title companies in setting up clients closing date, location and time.
This systematic training manual should provide you with enough Mortgage terms and skills needed to be successful in the Mortgage industry. Hands on training is always the best way to learn new skills, but after completing this manual you will be equipped with enough knowledge to get your foot in the door at ground level.

Excelling and working your way up, scoring the perfect position is entirely up to you!

The more steps you take, the further you go!

Please Note* This Training Manual is basic a little more than basic training, but does not guarantee the same system and techniques to every company and state… We take no responsibility for any information that does not apply to your state or company individually nor are we redeemed responsible for changes in the system or laws that apply to Home Mortgages and the financial lending system whatsoever. Laws, rules and changes are beyond our control and we advise you seek updates and changes from your local state and federal government such as Fannie Mae and Freddie Mac and other sources.

Summary

The majority of training manuals or home study courses consist of 100's of endless pages filling up space yet leaving the trainee in the state of confusion. The goal of our training manual is to simplify the training process breaking it down into 10 easy steps as well as to familiarize you with the major forms and terms used in the Mortgage Industry. You will find us a little redundant with important details at times and will find us pending some extra time and effort breaking down of the Loan Application. We'll do our best to be brief and getting to the point making it an enjoyable experience for you.

We feel confident that the simplicity of this training manual will become completely systematically in a short time. Soon you may find yourself on autopilot! (In a nutshell) If you have ever filled out an application for employment, it's not much different and even better, if you have applied for a mortgage home loan yourself you are already one step ahead of the training. During the process of applying for a home loan, credit card or employment, you know that there is numerous spaces that are provide for you to fill in your necessary personal information; the same techniques pretty much apply to your responsibilities as a loan processor, it's not your job to fill in the loan application, but it is to check all information concerning the loan applicant whether the be the buyer or just refinancing their current home.

By relating and referring to other similarities this training can become completely systematically and simplified. Let's use some prior experiences you may have had with filling out applications for employment, a lease contract, credit card, a car loan or perhaps even a mortgage home loan for yourself. Filling out these application, whatever their purpose, you know that you must fill in the blanks or the many spaces provided for personal information; the name, address, employment, social security number, dependents and so forth. The mortgage loan application consists of the same information necessary for helping the client/applicant/buyer get their loan approved and closed. The mortgage loan application is to be accurately and completely filled out by the client/applicant/buyer given to them by the loan officer this will be handed over to you in a file by that loan officer and you, as the loan processor, will begin to collect all the supporting documents to create a package to be sent to underwriting for loan approval and shortly after due process the loan will be closed.

Another example, if you were the attorney for a client, you would gather and checking information, interview client and prepare your case before presenting it before the judge. It would entail interviewing, make contacts, jotting down important notes and gathering information, collecting documents and preparing a solid case for your client to take to the jury. You would also pay close attention to the details of the case, the pro's and con's and be prepared to win after preparing the best accurate and complete case. This may sound complicated right now, but is there any job that the first few days you don't want to walk out and say, "I can't do this?" Believe me, you can do it!

On this page and the next, you will read the entire loan process and get a complete understanding of the process so you will understand where the loan processor's duties fit it, and how important your job is to this process.

The Complete Mortgage Loan Process

Note: These are the training to the mortgage loan in a nutshell.

From the time the buyer/borrower (or refinancing) seriously decides to purchase or refinance their Home to the closing of the loan, there are basically 7 steps.

First the borrower usually gets pre-qualified.

Step 1- Pre-qualified. (Before finding a home to purchase or before refinancing their current home)

Pre-qualification- before the home process begins, the buyer/borrower (refinance included) is pre-qualified. This is usually the first step after the contact is made with a Loan Officer. Note: not the Loan Processor. The loan originator gathers information on the prospect/borrower (s) concerning his or her income, pulls a credit report to view the debts and credit score. After all the information taken from the applicant has been reviewed, the Loan Officer makes a financial determination about how much house the borrower may be able to afford if qualified.
A verity of loan programs are offered to meet applicant's criteria

Step 2 – The Application
The "application" The true beginning of the loan process usually occurs within five business days of the pre-qualification... The buyer/borrower (Refinancing) completes a mortgage loan application with the loan officer required for processing.

Step 3 – Pre-Approval
Upon completion of application's information and credit report, the borrower with receive a pre-approval for his or her Mortgage Loan, at that time the file will be turned over to the Loan processor to complete

the collecting of the required documents and completing the file for underwriting.

Step 4- Processing
Processing begins as soon as you, the Loan Processor receive the file, usually 3 to 15 days from the time of the applicant/borrower being pre-approved. At this time you, the Processor, orders a property appraisal, orders and any other documents needed for processing of the loan. The borrower's <u>Completed File</u> is turned over to the lender for underwriting.

Step 5- Underwriting
Lender/ underwriting process takes between days 15 and 25. The underwriter is responsible for determining whether the combined package passed over by the processor is deemed as an acceptable loan. If more information is needed, the loan is put into "suspense" and the borrower is contacted to supply more documentation.

Step 6- Mortgage insurance.
When the borrower has less than 20% of the loan amount as a down payment. At this time, the loan is submitted to a private mortgage guaranty insurer, PMI Private Mortgage Insurance- provides extra insurance to the lender in case of default. Usually returned back to the mortgage company within 48 hours.

Step 7- Closing
Closing is the final step of the Home Mortgage Loan Process. The entire process usually takes about 30 days, some cases much quicker... At the closing table, the lender "funds" the loan with a cashier's check, draft or wire to the selling party in exchange for the title to the property. This is the point at which the borrower finishes the loan process and actually buys the house and receives the keys

NOTES: Always keep in mind, that different companies may require different rules- policies or stacking order.. Always refer to your company policies.

IMPORTANT NOTE: ALL BORROWER/APPLICANTION INFORMATION IS COMPLETELY CONFINDENTIAL AND CANNOT BE SHARED OR USED IN ANY WAY

*Helpful Hint

#1 --Form an automatic system
#2---Create a Conversation/tracking log (Mandatory)
#3 –Check All Forms (application and disclosures) for Signatures and Dates of all parties
#4—Keep each individual file neatly organized and handy

Note: When processing a mortgage loan Create a Conversation/tracking log in each file, this will enable you to keep track of what documents you have and those that you need to receive.

Most lenders require you to put the documents in what is know as a stacking order. The stacking order helps the underwriter look through your file with ease.
The <u>COMPLETED</u> file goes to the underwriter only after

1, Quickly order all required documents and conditions.

2, All completed documents have been collected (more on this later) Including Tracking Conversation Log

3, Documents that cannot be read legibly will not be acceptable and will delay the loan.

4, All Conditions have been met

5, Thoroughly check for all signatures and dates and

6, If the documents are grouped together in a certain order, the speed of your file being closed in a timely fashion is increased.

7, It is always a good idea to have the original documents available when requested by the lender.

8, Always remember to keep a copy of the file for your records. Some lenders have their own stacking order, but most will accept a file that's organized neatly by you. (more on this later)
9, Send only compete and signed files to lender

10, Mostly all documents you receive during the processes of the mortgage will come Loan Officer. It's very important that you make clean, eligible copies, with accurate information.

* ALL CHANGES TO BORROWER'S FILE MUST BE CAREFULLY NOTED AND LOGGED WITH BORROWER'S CHANGE FORM

Terms you should know

1, The Sales Contract --is not to be mistaken for the Loan Application
A contract between purchaser and a seller of real estate to convey title after certain conditions have been met. It is a form of installment sale.

2, The Loan Application contains crucial information.
Such as the borrower(s) name, signatures, street address, legal description, price, deposit amount, other properties the owner may have and other vital information used.

3. Mortgage Commitment: Send out within 3 days of Approval

A formal written notice from the bank or other lending institution stating the terms under which it agrees to lend mortgage funds to a homebuyer in a specified amount also known as a "loan commitment." commitment letter.

4. Loan Officer or Originator/Loan Processor Staff
Loan Origination: Refers to a person who is working directly with an applicant/borrower and conducting the basic underwriting analysis

- Steps a processor takes with a loan application

Collecting documents and information for underwriting to Purchase a house.
- Processing involves building a file of information for a loan. Processing includes getting the credit report, appraisal, verification of employment, assets, etc.

5, Loan Processor works with lender on building a file of information for the borrower's loan. Processing includes the ordering of the appraisal, verification of employment, assets, etc.

6, Loan Closing and funding
Home purchase, the process of transferring ownership from the seller to the buyer, the disbursement of funds from the seller and the lender to the buyer, and the execution of all the documents associated with the sale and the loan. On a refinance, there is no transfer of ownership, but the dosing includes repayment of the old lender

7, Underwriting- Underwriting involves the evaluation of the property as outlined in the appraisal report, and of the borrower's ability and willingness to repay the loan. The analysis of the risk involved in making a mortgage loan to determine whether the risk is acceptable to the lender.

Loan Closing and funding

- Home purchase, the process of transferring ownership from the seller to the buyer, the disbursement of funds from the seller and the lender to the buyer, and the execution of all the documents associated with the sale and the loan. On a refinance, there is no transfer of ownership, but the dosing includes repayment of the old lender.

8, Written agreement: to do or not to do a certain thing. Including Closing Date often referred to as the offer to purchase Home's Purchase Price

You will learn more about these terms in the following chapters

More terms you should know

1. Applicant- Uniform Residential Loan
Your Borrower (s) Personal Information, Credit and Employment History

2. Pre-Qualify- Pre-approval means the acceptance of the borrower's loan application. The borrower meets the lender and underwriter's requirements. In some or most cases, especially where approval is provided quickly. The approval may be conditional on further verification of information provided by the borrower.

3. Government Regulations- Some Loans are Government Loans such as VA and they require certain terms, rules and regulations. HUD information booklet explains the rights of the borrower under RESPA (Real Estate Settlement Procedure Act)
Full disclosure of settlement costs. Visit www.HUD.org or Freddie Mac.org

4. HUD 1 * also known as the "settlement sheet," it itemizes all closing costs;
This must be given to the borrower at or before closing.

5. Arm disclosure- Adjustable Rate Mortgages (ARMS)
A mortgage in which the interest rate can be changed by the lender after an initial period

6. ECOA- Equal Credit Opportunity Act

7. Sales Contract- Legal offer to Purchase (Realtor-buyer-seller)

8. TIL or Truth in Lending
- The law is designed to protect consumers in credit transactions by requiring clear disclosure of key terms of the lending arrangement and all costs.

9. Good Faith Estimate
- The form that lists the settlement charges the borrower must pay at closing which the lender is obliged to provide the borrower within three business days of receiving the loan application.

10. Credit Report- a report from a credit bureau containing detailed Information bearing on credit- worthiness including the individual's credit history.

11. Appraisal- A written estimate of a property's current market value prepared by an appraiser

12. Applicant Fee- the sum of all upfront cash payments required by the lender as part of the charge for the loan.

Introduction to loan processing

Purchasing or refinancing a home or investment property is probably be one of the biggest most important decision that hundreds of people make daily, and by becoming a Mortgage Loan Processor will make you a vital part of that decision. As a processor, you will have a great deal of interaction with the loan officer asking and answering questions, the underwriter and various companies such as title company, employers, etc. collecting and confirming document information and setting up an appointment for closing. One of your most important Jobs is the responsibility of moving buyer's information to the lender or underwriter as quickly and efficiently as possible.

A vast majority of individuals cannot afford to pay cash for their homes, which require them to apply for a home loan. As the Loan Processor you're role is a very important part in this process.

This first part of this guide explains the steps of mortgage processing. After completing this part, you should have a basic understanding of processing steps and be familiar with the terms so that you will be able to recognize and collect the appropriate documents and respond to the questions asked in processing a loan application.

As the Loan Processor, your job includes several crucial tasks. There are several basic steps to take in the processing of a Loan.

- Working closely with the Loan Officer providing clerical support
- Checking file for complete and accurate information concerning the loan
- Building a complete file of information and collecting necessary documents Identifying various loan types, forms, documents and supporting data
- Working with buyers on a timely schedule meeting Pre-Approval conditions

•Submitting complete accurate file to Underwriters
•Ordering Appraisal, title, Proof of Insurance, Set up buyers Closing date etc.
•Submitting the loan package to lender for approval

The beginning of a loan is the application, which usually is taken by the Loan Officer. This application should be submitted with the following information from the borrower. Employment and residency history, Income Source, Self Employed-additional documentation is required, Source of funds to be used Information on previous liens, bankruptcies, divorce, judgments, child support Assets, liabilities and any other property owned (if any) Type of loan (purchase or refinance)

Don't get scared, once you are familiar with the documents and ALL the ends and outs, it's easy.

First Contacts

Your most direct contact you will have with the borrower (s) is during your first encounter in which you take or examine the application and work with them on the conditions of the loan. Saving yourself time and aggravation later in your file or processing this loan make sure that the information taken from the borrower is accurate and complete and that they get you the required documents ASAP.

YOU SHOULD ALWAYS
* Provide information on loan requirements to applicant immediately
* Interview applicant and ask the Loan Officer questions to complete with accuracy all information on loan application
* Collect all necessary documents from borrower(s)
* Give a checklist of additional information he or she must provide ASAP

* Provide them with any literature, rate and other information concerning loan such as any government regulations, Arm disclosures, ECOA, truth in lending and the Good Faith Estimate
* Collect all monies for Credit Report, Appraisal and any application fee if applicable

Generally, the Loan Processor's are given the loan application with much of the information already taken by the Loan Officer. This file will come from the Loan Officer or sometimes referred to as the LO Immediately after receiving the loan application, you check the information and documents and begin preparing your file.

In preparation, you'll then need to know certain details and collect additional documents from the borrower (s) and other sources.
When you receive your file it should contain within it the Uniform Residential Loan Application (with all the important buyer information)

These are some of the files you will be collecting and making sure that are in the file before submitting it to underwriting. You'll learn all this in the following chapters!

- Disclosure Notices
- Lock in Conformation
- Agreements
- Requests Documents in your file from Loan Officer or LO
- Authorizations
- Letters and form

Let's begin

You just received your file from the Loan Officer or Originator.

The Mortgage Loan Processor generally follows TEN basic steps in the preparation of each file.

Company's requirements and state regulations may somewhat vary but every loan goes through the basic systematic procedures.

Origination — Prepares the loan application for the applicant or buyer. The loan originator collects the necessary information and documents from the applicant starting the loan process.

The Loan Processing or loan processor has a very crucial role in the loan — Checking and collecting the applicants supporting documents and preparing the loan for the underwriter. Without the processor's intervention (you), contacting and collecting all the necessary supporting documents the underwriter would not be able to approve the loan.

Conditions- Certain conditions are sometimes required before the applicant or buyer can obtain the loan therefore working with the borrower and other resources and point of contacts to obtain certain important pieces of information is vital to complete the file or loan package for the Underwriter.

Underwriting — Department where transactions undergo evaluation in order to approve and close a loan for a buyer or home refinancing — the final step for ownership and distribution of funds.

10 Basic Steps

Mortgage Loan Processors generally follow TEN basic steps in the preparation of a file

Keep in mind: Company's requirements may vary!
Every loan goes through the basic systematic procedures

1. Inquire of the Loan Officer is this Purchase or Refinancing
2. Inquire of the Loan Officer is this Full Documentation Loan or No Income
Verification Loan
3. Check, verify and enter loan application's information complete and accurate is vital
4. Obtain copy of sales contract
5. Copy of earnest check front and back
6. Request borrower's W2'S, Recent Pay Stubs
7. Obtain copies of 40 IK, IRA, Life Insurance (FACE VALUE)
8. Home Owners Insurance Binder and PMI
9. Order title and Appraisal
10. Check all information + documents and submit completed package/file to
Underwriting

The Loan Officer or Originator's Role

The beginning of the loan process is someone applying for a Mortgage loan from the lender or financial institution so they go to a loan officer or broker. The application is taken and parts of the borrower's information are hand written down on the application by the loan officer and then passed to you the Loan Processor.

The Processor's Role

The Processor is a vital key in the success of the loan with the exception of the borrower's cooperation and participation. Mortgage loan processing or the loan processor is one of the most important steps or roles in the processing of any loan. Being prompt, diligent and accurate are very important qualities needed to be a good and successful Loan Processor.
It is very important to inspect each document (Credit Report, VOD, VOE, Appraisal etc.)

* Ordering all necessary documentation quickly and efficiently.
* Reviewing the buyer's information and carefully checking for all signatures
* Verifying the borrower's information
* Ordering Verification of Deposit VOD
* Ordering Verification of Employment VOE
    - Ordering Appraisal and Title. (on a purchase.. Call Sellers attorney for title)

As well as ordering documents and much more

As you become familiar with these documents in the following chapters, you will learn exactly what information is required from you, the borrower, and other parties involved.

Being somewhat redundant will help you fully understand the documents and the process. In general, the mortgage processor collects, orders, checks and verifies the entire package given to them by the lender preparing and completing the borrowers file to close the loan.

Checking your file

You've just received your file from the Loan Officer or Originator
In your file, you should have been given the following documents.

1. Pre-approval for the loan
2. The credit report – Credit History
3. W2 or W2 s
4. Borrower (s) Pay Stubs
5. Signed Application
6. Disclosures
7. Usually a market annulus on an appraisal to see if the value is there before it became a loan
8. Only if Purchase *Sales Contract: Required prior to processing the loan

Note: A Sales Contract or Copy of it should be a part of the file given to you by the LO, if not, you can obtain the Signed Sales contract through the Realtor, Borrower or you can get the Borrower's Attorney's phone number and ask him or her for a copy of the signed document After receiving the sales contract, you will then need to check for the following *MUST BE SIGNED BY ALL PARTIES *

Documents you will need to order
*More on this in greater detail in the following chapters

Note: Again, keep in mind that each office may require different responsibility from the processor

1. Title (order first so you get it quickly) Ordering Appraisal and Title. (on purchase.. Call Sellers attorney for title)
2. Appraisal (order first so you get it quickly)
3. VOE -verification of employment
4. VOD -verification of deposit
5. VOR -verification of rent (if borrower was a renter)
6. Gift Letter (if borrower is receiving a financial gift)
7. Home Owners Insurance

Pay off if it's a refinance

SIVA : Stated income Verified Assets
SISA : Stated Income Stated Assets

Most companies you work for already have a preferred title and appraisal co they use for most if not all their loans

STEP 1,

You've just received your file from the Loan Officer or Originator Inquire of the Loan Officer is this Purchase or Refinancing.

*Note: Refinancing a home for the current owner may require less documentation depending upon circumstances.

Upon receiving your file, you should ask the Loan Officer if the Application is for the purpose of a purchase or Refinancing. The answer to these questions will determine what documentations are necessary for collection for the file. It's extremely imperative to familiarize yourself with the type of loan you are working with.

The Loan Application (WHICH OF THE TWO PURPOSES IS THE LOAN FOR?)
Purchase: The loan is used for the purchase of property
Refinance is the process of paying off one loan with the proceeds from a new loan using the same property as security. In Layman's Terms: To Get a Better Interest Rate, Cash Out or Other

If the application is for a purchase, you will then need to collect the following documents such as a complete copy of the sales contract from the borrower or borrower's realtor. Sales Contract: Required prior to processing the loan

MUST BE SIGNED BY ALL PARTIES *

• Written agreement: to do or not to do a certain thing. Including Closing Date
• Home's Purchase Price: often referred to as the offer to purchase.
• A contract between purchaser and a seller of real estate to convey title after certain conditions have been met. It is a form of installment sale.
• The Sales Contract is not to be mistaken for the Loan Application
The Loan Application contains crucial information.

Such as the borrower(s) name, signatures, street address, legal description, price, deposit amount, other properties the owner may have and other vital information used.

Check list of information to look for on the loan application

- Purpose of Loan - Subject Property address- property address being purchased
- Type of loan- Conventional, VA, FHA etc.
- Property Purchase amount
- Interest rate example 6.500 and is it fixed, ARM etc.
- No. Of months example 360
- Purchase or Refinance

Primary Residence (will they be living there, rental or investment)

No. Units (example Single family home)

Name or Names on title (example Mr. Borrower)

Social Security numbers of borrower(s)

All Financial information (Savings, Checking, IRS, 401K, Stocks, Bonds etc.)

All Borrower (s) information SS#, Address, Phone, Employment etc.

All Co-Borrowers information (if any) SS#, Address, Phone,

Employment etc Borrower's and

Co-Borrowers Employment information you receive your file from the

Quickly go over the Loan

Application and look for the items noted above.

Check and verify loan application's information making sure it's complete and accurate…
Completion and accuracy is a vital part of your job..

You can obtain the Signed Sales contract through the Realtor, Borrower or you can get the
Attorney's phone number and ask him or her for a copy of the signed document.

STEP 2

Income Documentation

FULL DOCUMENTATION LOAN or NO INCOME VERIFICATION LOAN

Terms to Study
1. Full DOC or Documentation— able to show all of your income
2. Stated or No Income Verification—stating an income without verification

In processing loans, you will experience various types of income and financial situations in each case you will be required to obtain different types of documents. There are two major income situations that you will become very familiar with full documentation and stated documentation. The two types also vary according to self-employed workers as opposed to wage earning workers. Full documentation refers to and individual being able to show all of their income- This will include; pay stub, W2, and Tax Returns. Stated documentation is stating an income without verifying it. No verification is needed for this type of documentation.

In order to begin your processing, there's one very important factor you must look for, is this applicant going to prefer a (Full Documentation or a Stated - No Income Verification) loan?

To determine this, the borrower must be able to provide you with proof of 2 years of income documents to cover their debts and mortgage

If your loan is going to be Full Documentation, you need to collect from the borrower. Company name and address with zip code.
 Note* Post office Box not acceptable Social Security number
Box on Loan application must be checked if Self Employed Borrower(s)
Complete Present Address VOE Verification of Employment
VOR (if) borrower is a renter will need 12 months of canceled rent checks
3 Months Bank Statements W2'S 2 Years of Federal Income Tax Returns Last 2 Most Recent Pay Stubs ALL INCOME INFORMATION 401K (If they have 401K plan) Gross income ERA (If they have an IRA) LIFE INSURANCE (FACE VALUE) All Real Estate Information AU Financial Information including

If the borrower(s) are going Stated or NO INCOME VERIFICATION here are the Documents that they must produce for you to complete the file, and get them their loan.

NIV

The No Income Verification (NIV) loan is perfect for those who cannot verify income with traditional documentation such as pay stubs or W-2 wage and tax statements. This type of loan is also referred to as a No Doc Loan. It is an excellent choice for people who are self-employed* The NIV Loan can used to purchase a home or refinance an existing mortgage. Documents to collect from borrower

- Employment information
- Company name and address with zip code. Note* Post office Box not acceptable
- Social Security number
- Box on Loan application must be checked (if Self Employed)
- Borrower(s) Complete Present Address
- Gross Monthly income amount
- VOD See Sample form Verification of Deposit
- VOE See Sample form Verification of Employment
- ALL Monthly Housing expense information

- All the information and documents above with the exception of Income.

NO income Verification: Loans does not require any income proof. *See below

All Financial Statements and other Supporting Documents

The Stated Income program provides applicants (with a strong credit and asset base) the ability to obtain home loans with no income verification and ratio calculation based on the income that the applicant discloses on the application. It is designed to meet the needs of applicants who have demonstrated a high regard for their financial obligations as evidenced by a minimum bureau score.

Current Employment (Salaried)
Income is stated on the application but not verified. Salaried borrowers must have a minimum of two years of continuous employment with the same employer or in the same line of work. Any employment change must be deemed career advancement. A verbal verification of employment confirming the following is required:

- Borrower's date of employment

- Borrower's employment status and job title
- Name, phone number and title of verifier
- Name and title of person making the call Current Employment (self-employed) require a signed IRS Form 4506 at submission (no exceptions).

- Self-employed borrowers must have a minimum of two years of continuous employment in the same line of work.
- Verification of the existence of the Borrower's business is required through evidence of a business license and confirmation of a phone directory listing. If a business license is not required the borrower's accountant or CPA requires a signed confirmation of the business.

NIV or (NO INCOME VERIFICATION) Your borrower cannot show proof of Income to cover their debt known as DTI. But they do earn enough money they will go Stated Income.

A debt-to-income ratio (often abbreviated DTI) is the percentage of a consumer's monthly gross income that goes toward paying debts. (Speaking precisely, DTI's often cover more than just debts; they can include certain taxes, fees and insurance premiums as well. Nevertheless, the term is a set phrase that serves as convenient and well-understood shorthand.) There are two main kinds of DTI, as discussed below.

Two main kinds of DTI
The two main kinds of DTI

First DTI, known as the front ratio, indicates the percentage of income that goes toward housing costs, which for renters is the rent amount and for homeowners is PITI (PITI includes mortgage principal and interest, mortgage insurance premium [when applicable], hazard insurance premium, property taxes, and homeowners association dues [when applicable]).

Second DTI, known as the back ratio, indicates the percentage of income that goes toward paying all recurring debt payments, including those covered by the first DTI, and other debts such as credit card payments, car loan payments, student loan payments, child support payments, alimony payments, and legal judgments.

Example

In order to qualify for a mortgage for which the lender requires a debt-to-income ratio of 28/36:
Yearly Gross Income = $45,000 / Divided by 12 = $3,750 per month income.
$3,750 Monthly Income x .28 = $1,050 allowed for housing expense.
$3,750 Monthly Income x .36 = $1,350 allowed for housing expense plus recurring debt.
Authorities seem to agree that a debt ratio (without a mortgage, utilities, etc.) of 10% or less is great. Debt ratios at 20% or higher are yellow lights as one emergency could topple the consumer.
Source of Down payment, Settlement charges or subordinate Financing Applicant must have adequate funds for the down payment and settlement costs. These funds must be verified and have an acceptable source.

Acceptable

• Verifiable monies, Saving, Liquid Investments, equity etc. Non-Acceptable
• Non Verifiable Money without paper trail
• Gifts from relatives providing entire down payment the buyer must have at least 3%
* Object to show they are reliable, responsible and able to afford the loan

STEP 3

Check and verify loan application's information making sure it's complete and accurate..
Completion and accuracy is a vital part of your job..

Check list of information to look for on the loan application

- Purpose of Loan - Subject Property address- property address being purchased
- Type of loan- Conventional, VA, FHA etc.
- Property Purchase amount
- Interest rate example 6.500 and is it fixed, ARM etc.
- No. Of months example 360
- Purchase or Refinance
- Primary Residence (will they be living there, rental or investment)
- No. Units (example Single family home)
- Name or Names on title (example Mr. Borrower)
- Social Security numbers of borrower(s)
- All Financial information (Savings, Checking, IRS, 401K, Stocks, Bonds etc.)

- All Borrower(s) information SS#, Address, Phone, Employment etc.

- All Co-Borrowers information (if any) SS#, Address, Phone, Employment etc Borrower's and

Co-Borrowers Employment information you receive your file from the Loan Officer or Originator Quickly go over the Loan
Application and look for the items noted above.

* MUST BE SIGNED BY ALL PARTIES *

STEP 4

Obtaining a copy of the Sales Contract

If the application is for a purchase, you will then need to collect the following documents such as a complete copy of the sales contract from the borrower or borrower's realtor. Sales Contract: Required prior to processing the loan

*MUST BE SIGNED BY ALL PARTIES

- Written agreement- to do or not to do a certain thing including the Closing Date.
- Often referred to as the Home's Purchase Price is an offer to purchase, it's a contract between purchaser and a seller of real estate to convey title after certain conditions have been met. It is a form of installment sale.
- The Sales Contract is not to be mistaken for the Loan Application

The Loan Application contains crucial information.
Such as the borrower(s) name, signatures, street address, legal description, price, deposit amount, other properties the owner may have and other vital information used.

STEP 5

Earnest Check Money- the buyer gives to a seller as part of the purchase price to bind a transaction or assure payment.

You will need a copy of the applicants Earnest Check that has already been deposited and cashed by the buyer's financial institution.

Understanding Earnest Money ...
So that you will not be placed in an uncomfortable position when you ask for a copy of the earnest check a greater understanding of the earnest money deposit is of great importance.

At the time a written offer on a property is initiated, the buyer will be required by the seller to include a personal or cashier's check for "earnest money".

Your buyer's money will be kept in the trust of the real estate company (or a designated title company) handling the listing and not turned over to the seller. Their deposit represents the sincerity in the attempt to purchase and it's refundable if the offer is not accepted, or if their loan(s) not approved, providing all the necessary dates are met in a timely manner.

When do they pay? They will submit earnest money with the purchase offer, anywhere from $1000 up.

The more expensive home the higher the earnest deposit. The amount is predetermined by the seller in the listing agreement with the listing agent and is published in the MLS. The amount like most elements of a contract is negotiable, however the more money they put down, the more serious their intent will appear to the seller.

This check will be held by the listing broker until contract agreement, at which time the check will be deposited into the listing broker (or title companies') trust account. The listing broker brings these funds to the closing.

It's extremely important that you receive a copy of both the front and backside of the Earnest Check

For collection of the Earnest Check, you will call the borrower for a copy to be mailed or faxed to you ASAP explaining to them that you need copy of both front and back of the Deposited and Cashed Check by the financial institution.

STEP 6

Request borrower's W2'S, Recent Pay Stubs
W2'S 2 Years of Federal Income Tax Returns Last 2 Most Recent Pay Stubs ALL INCOME INFORMATION

Current Employment (Salaried)
Income is stated on the application but not verified. Salaried borrowers must have a minimum of two years of continuous employment with the same employer or in the same line of work. Any employment change must be deemed career advancement. A verbal verification of employment confirming the following is required:

- Borrower's date of employment
- Borrower's employment status and job title
- Name, phone number and title of verifier
- Name and title of person making the call Current Employment (self-employed) require a signed IRS Form 4506 at submission (no exceptions).

NIV or (NO INCOME VERIFICATION) Your borrower cannot show proof of Income to cover their debt known as DTI. But they do earn enough money they will go Stated Income.

No Income Verification Loan (NIV) also known as Stated Income - requires No W2's, No Pay stubs, No Tax returns, and No IRS Forms. Available to W-2 wage earners, 1099, Self Employed, and Retired.

Stated Income Verified Assets Loan: (SIVA) - Loan approval is based on your stated income, credit history, and verified liquid assets. The Verified Assets should be consistent with the income claimed.

The Stated Income program provides applicants (with a strong credit and asset base) the ability to obtain home loans with no income verification and ratio calculation based on the income that the applicant discloses on the application. It is designed to meet the needs of applicants who have demonstrated a high regard for their financial obligations as evidenced by a minimum bureau score

STEP 7

Obtain copies of 40 IK, IRA, Life Insurance (FACE VALUE)

ALL INCOME INFORMATION 401K (If they have 401K plan) Gross income ERA (If they have an IRA) LIFE INSURANCE (FACE VALUE) All Real Estate Information AU Financial Information including

STEP 8

Home Owners Insurance Binder and PMI

Mortgage Insurance

Home Owners Insurance Binder (DEC PACE) With Paid Receipt The borrower(s) will need to hold Home Owners Insurance Known as a DEC Page or Binder
This Document is from the borrowers Insurance Company.
This DEC page must show that the borrowers are covered for the FULL amount of their new loan.

*Usually Requires the PAID IN FULL RECEIPT FOR 12 MONTHS *
Shows the Lender that this has been purchased and paid in full and how it was paid. Confirm with Lender for each loan type.

The Processor will need to get the Name and Phone Number of the Borrowers
Insurance Company

PMI

Typically, banks require homeowners to obtain private mortgage insurance (PMT) if they are putting down less than 20 percent of a home's value at the time of purchase. On a $100,000 mortgage, the monthly costs for PMI would range from S30-S75 depending on the size of the down payment.

If Borrowers don't have an Insurance Company you will need to inform them that they are required to purchase Insurance for the entire year in advance on their purchased property before they can close their loan. All lenders have their own mortgage Clause that will be added to the insurance such as the lenders name, address etc. You will need to get all this information from the lender.

Mortgage insurance (MI)- Insurance written by an independent mortgage insurance company protecting the mortgage lender against loss incurred by a mortgage default - * Usually required for loans with an LTV of 80.01% or higher.

Private mortgage insurance (PMI)
Insurance provided by nongovernmental insurers that protect lenders against loss if a borrower defaults. Fannie Mae generally requires private mortgage insurance for loans with loan-to-value (LW) percentages greater than 80%.

STEP 9

Ordering Appraisal and Title

Appraisal must be ordered and acceptable by the underwriters for approval.

View the sample appraisal in this chapter for the information you need to check.

The Appraisal Document is extremely important part of the loan processing. The Appraisal determines the Value of the Subject Property. If they Subject Properties appraisal Value is not equal or greater than the amount of Purchase; the loan will not be approved.

The majority of Mortgage Companies have appraisers they use often. This is optional and varies from lender to lender.

Terms to familiarize

1. Appraisal - A written analysis of the estimated value of a property prepared by a qualified appraiser.
Estimated or opinion of the fair market value of the subject property.

2. Appraiser - A person qualified by education, training, and experience to estimate the value of real property and personal property.

3. Appraisal Reports - Refer to sample documents included in this manual

ORDERING THE TITLE

The Processor will request the (seller's Attorney) phone number from the realtor and call the sellers attorney to obtain the title.

If the Loan is for refinancing the subject property, the Processor will order the title. The title must have borrowers NAME on it and cannot have any Liens, nor can it be in the process of foreclosure. The effective date on the title must be less than 60 days.

Terms to familiarize

1. Title * The evidence one has of right to possession of land.

2. Title insurance -Insurance against loss resulting from defects of title to a specifically described parcel of real property.

3. Title search - An investigation into the history of ownership for the property to check for liens, unpaid claims, restrictions or problems. To prove that the seller can transfer property ownership free and clear.

4. Certificate of title- A statement provided by an abstract company, title company, or attorney stating that the title to real estate is legally held by the current owner.

5. Chain of title- the history of all of the documents that transferred title to a parcel of real property starting with the earliest existing document and ending with the most recent.

6. Clear title- a title that is free of liens or legal questions as to ownership of the property.

7. Deed- the legal document conveying title to a property.

8. Deed-in-lieu- A deed given by a mortgagor to the mortgagee to satisfy a debt avoiding foreclosure.

9. Deed of trust* the document used in some states instead of a mortgage; title is conveyed to a trustee.

Refer to Sample Documents included in this manual

Ordering Other Supporting Documents

Since your job entails collection of Documents and preparing the file or case, so to speak, it's a good idea to keep close contact with the lender, the Loan Officer and underwriting to make sure you have collected all the documentation that is required to close this loan

Gift Letter

See Sample Document
What is a gift letter?

A Parent or other relative may be willing to make a gift of funds in order for the buyer to purchase a home, lenders will ask for a gift letter stating that no repayment of the "gift" is expected. The amount of the gift and the date funds were transferred should be spelled out in the letter, along with the donor's name, address, telephone number and relationship to the borrower.

In addition to the letter, a lender can ask for two or three months' worth of statements for the account where the down payment funds are located. If the money was recently placed into that account, the lender may ask where it came from and request verification of that source as well. Lenders often have stricter restrictions on gifts from friends and relatives other than parents. Note: Less than 20 percent down, some lenders may require that a portion of the down payment be your own cash, not a gift

Step 10

Check all information + documents and submit completed package/file to Underwriting

Basic Applicant Interview or Questions

- How is their credit and credit history?
- Do they have enough assets to cover loan?
- Is Income adequate and stable enough to meet this obligation?

For various reasons, applicants often provide incomplete information during the Interview or on their application.
Lenders need to verify the record only facts for each loan to be approved.

The purpose of supporting documents is to provide the lender with accurate information so that a good evaluation of a loan status can be determined. The VOE, VOD, VOR, Sales Contract, Credit Report and other credit documentations are collected and evaluated and the decision is handed down to the borrower(s)

Other Documents that may be required to meet conditions

VOE- Verification of Employment
A document signed by the borrower's employer verifying his/her position and salary.

VOD- Verification of Deposit

A document signed by the borrower's financial institution verifying the status and balance of his/her financial accounts
Divorce Papers

Why divorce papers?
This is to reassure the lender there are no out standing debts, alimony or child support from a previous marriage owed by the applicant. They must be included in the debt ratio calculations.

If the applicant will use alimony or child support as income to support the new mortgage, receipts of the payment for at least a year must be verified by court records or cancelled checks. If an applicant is divorced, you should examine both the divorce papers and separation agreement to see the full financial obligations.

Separation Agreements: Treated like divorce papers.

Conditions   Fulfilling All Conditions

When the Processor receives the file from the lender, there is conditions that must fulfilled before the borrower to be approved and get their loan close. These Conditions must be collected by the Processor and Submitted to the Lender as a complete package and not piece-by-piece or document-by-document. Your Main Office will also need a Complete a copy of the file and require it in a certain order. Most Offices have their own stacking order.
Why Conditional Loan Approval?

Your borrowers mortgage loan will most likely be approve by the loan agent or mortgage broker, be sure to ask if there are any conditions that must be met. Most mortgages are approved subject to certain conditions being satisfied before closing. The borrower(s) loan is approved as long as they can satisfy the lender's requirements. If they can't, they won't get their loan.

Some of the conditions will be easy to satisfy, like providing a legible copy of the purchase contract. The lender might need verification of some of financial documentation, such as a copy of the gift letter from their parents or other relative, or a signed copy of their most recent Income tax returns. The lender might want proof that they paid down or off a charge card account, or that they liquidated stock for part of the down payment Buyers whose down payment is coming from the sale of another property will probably be required to provide the lender with a "HUD-1" from the sale of that property.

A HUD-1 is a settlement sheet that shows the net proceeds from the sale. Lenders need to verify the source of the buyers' down payment funds before they will grant a loan.

All conditions on the approval must be collected by you, the processor, and submitted to the lender as a complete package not piece by piece your main office will need a complete copy of the file also and in their stacking order; usually every offices has their own stacking order just as all banks have tellers that service your transactions, but each bank has it's own processing rules and fees.

Once all conditions have been cleared it is time to arrange for the closing if refi the processor will call title co and borrowers to set up the closing if purchase the closing has already been set up by the selling attorney once closed it is processors responsibility to get the hud-1 or settlement statement by calling the closing location example the attorneys office or the title company to carefully examine the hud-1 before the borrowers get to the closing office to make sure all fees are accurate. Once the HUD-1 has been signed by all parties arrange for the broker check to be picked up or delivered.

- Call for the 1st hud-1 from closing location to be faxed to you
- Carefully examine the hud-1 for any errors such inaccurate fees
- Once all the fees are correct tell the closer to fax you a copy of the final signed

HUD-1 which should be signed by both the borrower/s and the closer
• Depending on your office regulations or your duties, you may need to arrange the brokers check to be picked up or delivered to your office
• Once you receive the signed hud-1, you will place this hud-1 in your "Now" completed and closed file at this point you will turn over the completed closed file to your broker once the funds have cleared you will be paid according to the agreement between the broker and yourself.

THIS FILE IS NOW CLOSED.

Quick Recap

Duties of a processor
Upon receiving the file you will need to know the following

1. Is it a purchase or a refinance if purchase you will need copy of sales contract signed by all parties, copy of back and front of deposit earnest check

2. Is this a full documentation loan if so, these documents will be needed
•   3 months bank statements, W2's for the last 2 years, last 2 most recent pay stubs, any

other 401k etc.
3. Regardless of refi or purchase you will need homeowners insurance, with paid in full receipt. All lenders have a mortgage eclause that will be added to the insurance such as the lenders name, address

4. Appraisal must be ordered and acceptable to underwriter's approval

5. Title most be ordered by processor if refi if a purchase the processor will call selling attorney to get title, the title must have borrowers name on it and can not have any leans on it nor can it be in foreclosure and the effective date on title must be less than 60 days old

6. All conditions on the approval must be collected by processor and submitted to the lender as a complete package not piece by piece your main office will need a complete copy of the file also and in their stacking order all offices usually have their own stacking order

7. Once all conditions have been cleared, it's time to arrange for the closing.
If refi (refinancing) the processor will call the title company and the borrowers to set up
the closing.

(If purchase) the closing has already been set up by the setting attorney
* Always check with all parties to verify all information about closing as well as other information.

Once closed it is you the processor's responsibility to get the HUD-1 or settlement statement and arrange for the broker's check to be picked up or delivered.

This file is now closed.

Understanding The Credit Report

Understanding Credit Report

Understanding Credit Report and Fico Scores.

Credit is more than a report: it also determines an applicants' eligibility if any, and the rate they qualify for. Although there are many programs that): meet almost everyone's need, Good Credit is so important. The Credit Report is the key in determining the borrower's creditworthiness. Borrower' credit report tells current and past history, along with the credit scores know as FICO. Term you know. The Fico scores are used in conjunction with other important documents and information to determine if the borrower will qualify for a mortgage loan. When using credit report to determine qualification, most lenders order an INfile. Term you should know.

INfile- There are 3 major credit reporting Bureau's
- 1, Equifax
- 2, Experian
- 3, TransUnion

When credit information is ordered from only one of these Credit Bureau's an INfile will only disclose information reported to that particular Bureau by a creditor, along with the borrower's credit scores. This is very minimal information due to the fact that some creditors may report a borrower's creditworthiness and credit history to two Bureaus whereas some may report to all three. To fully know the borrower's full credit history, lenders will usually require all three Credit Reporting Bureaus.

The 3 Credit Bureaus will disclose all credit history information pertaining to the borrower along with the fico scores from each bureau.

Elements of the Credit Report

New Loans: Check the new loan, can the borrowers afford this new debt? Is the loan secured or unsecured? Was the loan intended for down payment purposes?

Payment History: Derogatory credit should be explained thoroughly by the borrower(s) in a credit letter. This requirement applies to the individual credit verifications

Credit Explanation: In receiving explanations, it's your decision whether the explanation is reasonable. Do the facts presented coincide with the borrowers story (divorce decree, paid receipts, etc.)? Was it a one-time incident (medical), or do you see a continual pattern of delinquencies that may continue in the future?

Public Records: These records show any judgments, collections, bankruptcies, and suits. The borrower must satisfy any of these outstanding debts.

Recent Inquiries: The borrower must explain in writing the nature of any listed Inquiries. If any debt has incurred as a result of an inquiry and is not on the credit report, a separate verification should be obtained

Credit Scores: Generally, a minimum of two credit bureau scores should be obtained on each borrower. When underwriting a case with two scores, you should rely upon the lowest of the two scores. If there are three scores, you should rely upon the middle score. You should also review the Reason Codes provided with the credit bureau score(s). These will allow you to see the areas of a borrower credit profile that impacted the score. Finally, remember when pulling scores from the repositories that there can be regional differences in the INfile data used to score the borrower. It would be a good idea to adopt a Preferred Repository List to assist in directing you to the most appropriate repository for that borrower. This is usually done by zip code.

If you, the lender, must decline the loan because of information found in a credit report, you must give the borrower a written reason for denial and the name of the credit reporting agency furnishing the report

Other Support Documents

The applicant may foe required to provide documentation on any of the following depending on personal circumstances

- Divorce Papers
- Separation Agreements

For the purpose of finding out if there may be any outstanding debts, alimony, or child support from a previous marriage owed by the applicant? They must be included in the debt ratio calculations.

If the applicant will use alimony or child support as income to support the new mortgage, receipt of the payments for at east a year must be verified by court records or canceled checks.

If an applicant is divorced, you should examine both the divorce papers and separation agreement to see the full financial obligations. These can be treated like divorce papers, but remember that the amounts may be subject to changes before the divorce s final.

An applicant whose divorce is not final should be treated very conservatively when applying for a mortgage.

In a community property state, the applicant may not be aware that the separated spouse will own half of the newly purchased property if the divorce is not final at closing

APPLICANT	Mr. Borrower		CO-APPLICANT:	
SOC SEC #:		AGE:	SOC SEC #:	AGE:
STREET:	1234 Need Lane		YEARS AT ADDR.:	
CITY, STATE, ZIP:	All USA... 12345		MARITAL STATUS:	# OF DEP.:

EMPLOYMENT INFORMATION

EMPLOYER:			EMPLOYER:		
POSITION:			POSITION:		
SINCE:		INCOME:	SINCE:		INCOME:
VERIFIED BY:			VERIFIED BY:		

CREDITOR ACCT NO	ECOA	DATE OPENED	STATUS DATE / LAST ACTIVE	HIGHEST CREDIT OR LIMIT	APPROX. BALANCE / AMT PAST DUE	TERMS	HISTORICAL STATUS: TIME PAST DUE 30/60/90	DATE LAST PAST DUE	CURRENT STATUS / MONTHS REPORTED

SCORE MODELS

1 Mr. Borrower 123-4-5678
EQUIFAX/BEACON   582
00038 - SERIOUS DELINQUENCY, AND DEROGATORY PUBLIC RECORD OR COLLECTION FILED
00013 - TIME SINCE DELINQUENCY IS TOO RECENT OR UNKNOWN
00014 - LENGTH OF TIME ACCOUNTS HAVE BEEN ESTABLISHED
00016 - LACK OF RECENT REVOLVING ACCOUNT INFORMATION

3 Mr. Borrower 123-4-5678
TRANSUNION/EMPIRICA   526
038 - SERIOUS DELINQUENCY, AND PUBLIC RECORD OR COLLECTION FILED
018 - NUMBER OF ACCOUNTS WITH DELINQUENCY
002 - LEVEL OF DELINQUENCY ON ACCOUNTS
020 - LENGTH OF TIME SINCE DEROGATORY PUBLIC RECORD OR COLLECTION IS TOO SHORT

2 Mr. Borrower 123-4-5678
EXPERIAN/FAIR, ISAAC (VER. 2)   534
38 - SERIOUS DELINQUENCY AND PUBLIC RECORD OR COLLECTION FILED
18 - NUMBER OF ACCOUNTS DELINQUENT
02 - DELINQUENCY REPORTED ON ACCOUNTS
14 - LENGTH OF TIME ACCOUNTS HAVE BEEN ESTABLISHED

PUBLIC RECORDS
*** NO RECORD FOUND ***

OPEN ACCOUNTS
*** NO RECORD FOUND ***

CLOSED ACCOUNTS

GAS   B 07/02 04/03 $0 $0 $0   0 0 0   I1
853060   10/02 $0 PAID   01
TU3
ACCOUNT CLOSED BY CONSUMER; UTILITY COMPANY

DEROGATORY ACCOUNTS

COLLECTION COMPANY   B 09/00 10/00 $398 $398 UNK $-   09
XP2 $398 COLLECTION   1
ORIGINAL CREDITOR: FACC NEW YORK

Paid

ECOA KEY: B=BORROWER; C=CO-BORROWER; S=SHARED; J=JOINT; U=UNDESIGNATED; A=AUTHORIZED USER

APPLICANT					CO-APPLICANT			
APPLICANT: Mr. Borrower		AGE:			CO-APPLICANT:		AGE:	
SOC SEC #:					SOC SEC #:			
STREET: 1234 Need Lane					YEARS AT ADDR.:		# OF DEP.:	
CITY, STATE, ZIP: All USA... 12345					MARITAL STATUS:			

CREDITOR ACCT NO.	ECOA	DATE OPENED	STATUS DATE LAST ACTIVE	HIGHEST CREDIT OR LIMIT	APPROX BALANCE AMT PAST DUE	TERMS	HISTORICAL STATUS TIME PAST DUE 30/60/90	DATE LAST PAST DUE	CURRENT STATUS MONTHS REPORTED
CREDIT PROTECTION EF1/XP2/TU3 ORIGINAL CREDITOR: HOLLYWOOD VIDEO, ASSIGNED ON 11/00	B	11/00	06/02 08/00	$146	$146 $146	UNK $146 COLLECTION *Paid*			09
CRED PROTECTIONS AS ORIGINAL CREDITOR: AT&T BROADBAND	B	08/02	10/02	$50	$0 $0	UNK $0 PAID COLL			09 2
G M A C Late Dates: 11/00-30, 10/00-30	B	01/10/2000	09/02	$13389	$0 $0	060 $0 PD WAS 60	10 1 0	11/00	I1 58
GAS Late Dates: 6/02-30, 10/00-120, 8/00-90, 7/00-60, 6/00-30 CLOSED; UTILITY COMPANY	B	01/00	08/02 07/02	$0	$0 $0	$0 PD WAS 30	2 1 2	06/02	I1 30
ACCT MGMT ORIGINAL CREDITOR:	B	07/02	03/02	$60	$0 $0	UNK $0 PAID COLL			09 1
FINANCIAL Late Dates: 2/03-30, 8/02-120, 7/02-90, 6/02-60, 5/02-30 ACCOUNT CLOSED AT CREDIT GRANTOR'S REQUEST	B		12/02	$606	$0 $0	$0 PD WAS 120	2 1 2	02/03	R1 18
FCU 220000/ TU3 Late Dates: 5/00-30 ACCOUNT CLOSED BY CONSUMER	B	10/99	04/02 09/01	$588	$0 $0	$0 PD WAS 30	1 0 0	05/00	R1 14

INQUIRIES

*** NO RECORD FOUND ***

CREDITORS

COLLECTION COMPANY OF	700 LONGWATER DR,
CRED PROTECTIONS ASSOC	1355 NOEL RD SUITE 2100,
CREDIT PROTECTION	355 NOEL ROAD#,
CREDIT INK	29W110 BUTTERFIELD S
G M A C	200 N EXECUTIVE
GMAC.	P O BOX 100049,
GAS	1844 FERRY ROAD
ACCT MGMT IN	2040 W WISCONSIN
FINANCIAL	PO BOX 9180, PLEA

ECOA KEY: B=BORROWER; C=CO-BORROWER; S=SHARED; J=JOINT; U=UNDESIGNATED; A=AUTHORIZED USER

29 W 110　　　　　　　　　　　**◉ Credit　ink**　　　　Phone: (800) 588-1234
Suite 105　　　　　　　　　　　　　　　　　　　　　　　　　　Fax: (822) 393-9325
San Ana CA. 92102

CREDIT REPORT

FILE #:	410738	REISSUE #:	REQUESTED BY:	DOROTHY SONTON		
PREPARED FOR:	AMERICAN FUNDS		LOAN TYPE:		DATE ORDERED:	02-30-2008
			REPOSITORIES:	XP/TU/EF	REPORT DATE:	
			LOAN #:		PRICE:	$11.00

APPLICANT		CO-APPLICANT	
APPLICANT:	Mr. Borrower	CO-APPLICANT:	
SOC SEC #:		SOC SEC #:	AGE:
STREET:	1234 Need Lane	YEARS AT ADDR.:	
CITY, STATE, ZIP:	All USA... 12345	# OF DEP.:	
		MARITAL STATUS:	

CREDITOR ACCT NO.	ECOA	DATE OPENED	STATUS DATE LAST ACTIVE	HIGHEST CREDIT OR LIMIT	APPROX BALANCE AMT PAST DUE	TERMS	HISTORICAL STATUS TIME PAST DUE / DATE LAST PAST DUE	CURRENT STAT MONTHS REPOR

==
　　　　　　　　　　　　S O U R C E　　O F　　I N F O R M A T I O N
==

1 - EQUIFAX 02-30-2008
　NAME: Mr. Borrower
　SSN: 123-45-6789
　ADDRESS: 1234 Need Lane, ALL USA 12345
　EMPLOYER: Federal Reserve

2 - EXPERIAN 02-30-2008
　NAME: Mr. Borrower
　SSN: 123-45-6789
　ADDRESS: 123 Im Renting way, City Life, NY   09/02
　ADDRESS: 456 my city apartment Country side, NY 09/97

3 - TRANSUNION 02-30-2008
　NAME: Mr. Borrower
　NAME: DOB 12-15-1989
　SSN:
　ADDRESS: 123 Im Renting way, City Life, NY   03/03
　ADDRESS: 456 my city apartment Country side, NY 3 05/01
　ADDRESS:

==
　　　　　　　　　　　M I S C E L L A N E O U S　　I N F O R M A T I O N
==

Instant View Password: 3A1B3

Fannie User ID: ASAP1134

To verify the authenticity of this credit report, please visit
https://creditstinks.com   and click on the Instant View link. Enter report
number XXXX and password XXXX to view the report. For any inquiries regarding
this report or services provided by CREDIT INK please contact us at 1800 123-call   .

Dear Homebuyer,
　　　This In-file Credit Report contains credit and public records information that
has been obtained from the credit repositories listed above. Duplicate information
may exist. Payoffs, update tradelines, and verification of information may not be
included in this report.

　　　While this report may be used for real estate lending purpose, it is not
considered a Residential Mortgage Credit Report as defined by FNMA, PHLMC, and FHA/VA
guidelines.

　　　If further verification by Credit Link is required, investigation fees may apply.
This in-file credit report may be converted, by the mortgage lender, to a
Residential Mortgage Credit Report within 30 days.

　　　　　　　　　　　　　　　　*** END OF REPORT 02-30-2008 2:03:53 PM ***

EQUAL CREDIT OPPORTUNITY ACT

APPLICATION NO.   MR. BORROWER   Date: 02/28/08

PROPERTY ADDRESS   123 JOHN ST
                   JOHNSTOWN, NY 12345

The Federal Equal Credit Opportunity Act prohibits creditors from discriminating against credit applicants on the basis of race, color, religion, national origin, sex, marital status, age (provided the applicant has the capacity to enter into a binding contract); because all or part of the applicant's income derives from any public assistance program; or because the applicant has in good faith exercised any right under the Consumer Credit Protection Act. The Federal Agency that administers compliance with this law concerning this company is the Comptroller of the Currency Customer Assistance Group, 1301 McKinney Street, Suite 3450 Houston, Texas 77010-9050

We are required to disclose to you that you need not disclose income from alimony, child support or separate maintenance payment if you choose not to do so.

Having made this disclosure to you, we are permitted to inquire if any of the income shown on your application is derived from such a source and to consider the likelihood of consistent payment as we do with any income on which you are relying to qualify for the loan for which you are applying.

_____   _____
SAMPLE ONLY BORROWER (Applicant)   (Date)   (Applicant)   (Date)

_____   _____
           (Applicant)   (Date)   (Applicant)   (Date)

CREDIT SCORE DISCLOSURE/NOTICE TO THE HOME LOAN APPLICANT

DATE: _____   LOAN NUMBER: _____

APPLICANT NO. 1: _____

APPLICANT NO. 2: _____

MAILING
ADDRESS: _____

APPLICANT NO. 1

The credit score of Applicant No. 1 is _____. This credit score was created _____ (Date).

The credit score was provided by: _____ Equifax _____ TransUnion _____ Experian

The following factor(s) adversely affected the credit score of Applicant No. 1: (*Code #) _____, _____, _____, _____

APPLICANT NO. 2

The credit score of Applicant No. 2 is _____. This credit score was created _____ (Date).

The credit score was provided by: _____ Equifax _____ TransUnion _____ Experian

The following factor(s) adversely affected the credit score of Applicant No. 2: (*Code #) _____, _____, _____, _____

The possible credit scores under the scoring used by Equifax range from a low of 300 to a high of 850.
The possible credit scores under the scoring used by Trans Union range from a low of 395 to a high of 848.
The possible credit scores under the scoring used by Experian range from a low of 375 to a high of 900.

The factors contributing to your credit score are only one of the many factors we use in determining whether or not to grant credit. This Notice is not a notice of the action taken on your loan. This Notice may or may not contain the reason(s) for our decision on your application. You will receive a formal decision on your application at a later date.

See attached for explanation of codes and address and telephone number information for Equifax, TransUnion and Experian.

NOTICE

IN CONNECTION WITH YOUR APPLICATION FOR A HOME LOAN, THE LENDER/BROKER MUST DISCLOSE TO YOU THE SCORE THAT A CONSUMER REPORTING AGENCY (ALSO KNOWN AS A CREDIT BUREAU) DISTRIBUTED TO USERS AND THE LENDER/BROKER USED IN CONNECTION WITH YOUR HOME LOAN, AND THE KEY FACTORS AFFECTING YOUR CREDIT SCORES.

THE CREDIT SCORE IS A COMPUTER GENERATED SUMMARY CALCULATED AT THE TIME OF THE REQUEST AND BASED ON INFORMATION A CONSUMER REPORTING AGENCY OR LENDER/BROKER HAS ON FILE. THE SCORES ARE BASED ON DATA ABOUT YOUR CREDIT HISTORY AND PAYMENT PATTERNS. CREDIT SCORES ARE IMPORTANT BECAUSE THEY ARE USED TO ASSIST THE LENDER/BROKER IN DETERMINING WHETHER YOU WILL OBTAIN A LOAN. THEY MAY ALSO BE USED TO DETERMINE WHAT INTEREST RATE YOU MAY BE OFFERED ON THE MORTGAGE. CREDIT SCORES CAN CHANGE OVER TIME, DEPENDING ON YOUR CONDUCT, HOW YOUR CREDIT HISTORY AND PAYMENT PATTERNS CHANGE AND HOW CREDIT SCORING TECHNOLOGIES CHANGE.

BECAUSE THE SCORE IS BASED ON INFORMATION IN YOUR CREDIT HISTORY, IT IS VERY IMPORTANT THAT YOU REVIEW THE CREDIT-RELATED INFORMATION THAT IS BEING FURNISHED TO MAKE SURE THAT IT IS ACCURATE. CREDIT RECORDS MAY VARY FROM ONE COMPANY TO ANOTHER.

IF YOU HAVE QUESTIONS ABOUT YOUR CREDIT SCORE OR THE CREDIT INFORMATION THAT IS FURNISHED TO YOU, CONTACT THE CONSUMER REPORTING AGENCY AT THE ADDRESS AND TELEPHONE NUMBER PROVIDED WITH THIS NOTICE, OR CONTACT THE LENDER/BROKER. IF THE LENDER/BROKER DEVELOPED OR GENERATED THE CREDIT SCORE. THE CONSUMER REPORTING AGENCY PLAYS NO PART IN THE DECISION TO TAKE ANY ACTION ON THE LOAN APPLICATION AND IS UNABLE TO PROVIDE YOU WITH SPECIFIC REASONS FOR THE DECISION ON A LOAN APPLICATION.

IF YOU HAVE QUESTIONS CONCERNING THE TERMS OF THE LOAN, CONTACT THE LENDER/BROKER.

Please acknowledge your receipt of this Notice by signing below.

_____   _____
Applicant   Date

_____   _____
Applicant   Date

FACTA Credit Notice
Revised: 11/19/04

Fair Isaac Credit Bureau Risk Scoring Factor Reason Codes

Reason Statement	Equifax (Beacon)	Trans Union (Empirica)	Experian (Fico II)
Amounts owed on accounts is too high	01	01	A/01
Level of delinquency on accounts	02	02	B/02
Too few bank revolving accounts			C/03
Proportion of loan balances to loan amounts is too high	33	33	I/33
Too many bank or national revolving accounts	04		D/04
Lack of recent installment loan information	32	04	Y/32
Too many accounts with balances	05	05	E/05
Too many consumer finance accounts	06	06	F/06
Account payment history is too new to rate	07	07	G/07
Too many inquiries last 12 months	08	08	H/08
Too many accounts recently opened	09	09	J/09
Proportion of balance to credit limits too high on bank revolving or other revolving accounts	10	10	K/10
Amount owed on revolving accounts is too high	11	11	L/11
Length of time revolving accounts have been established	12	12	M/12
Time since delinquency too recent or unknown	13	13	N/13
Length of time accounts have been established	14	14	O/14
Lack of recent bank revolving information	15	15	P/15
Lack of recent revolving account information	16	16	Q/16
No recent non-mortgage balance information	17	17	R/17
Number of accounts with delinquency	18	18	S/18
Too few accounts currently paid as agreed	19	27	T/19
Date of last inquiry too recent		19	
Length of time since derogatory public record or collection is too short	20	20	V/20
Amount past due on accounts	21	21	W/21
Number of bank or national revolving accounts with balances	23		
No recent revolving balances	24	24	U/24
Length of time installment loans have been established			36
Number of revolving accounts			26
Number of established accounts	28	28	28
No recent bankcard balances		29	
Time since most recent account opening is too short	30	30	Z/30
Too few accounts with recent payment information	31		31
Amount owed on delinquent accounts	34	31	34
Length of time open installment loans have been established			36
Number of consumer finance company accounts established relative to length of consumer finance history			37
Serious delinquency and public record or collection filed	38	38	X/38
Serious delinquency	39	39	X/39
Derogatory public record or collection filed	40	40	X/40
Lack of recent auto loan information			98
Length of time consumer finance company loans have been established		98	
Lack of recent auto loan information		97	
Lack of recent consumer finance company account information			99

Equifax: Credit Bureau of Greensboro, P.O. Drawer A, Greensboro, NC 27402 (800) 378-2732
Trans Union: Trans Union Credit Corporation, P.O. Box 390, Springfield, PA 19064 (800) 888-4213
Experian: Experian Information Services, P.O. Box 2002, Allen, TX 75013 (800) 397-3742

THE HOUSING FINANCIAL DISCRIMINATION ACT OF 1977
FAIR LENDING NOTICE

DATE: 01/01/2000

APPLICATION NO: MR.BORROWER

PROPERTY ADDRESS: 123 JOHN ST
JOHNSTOWN, NY 12345

COMPANY: YOUR LENDING CO
113 JOHN ST
BLOOMINGTON, NY 111111

It is illegal to discriminate in the provisions of or in the availability of financial assistance because of the consideration of:

1. Trends, characteristics or conditions in the neighborhood or geographic area surrounding a housing accommodation, unless the financial institution can demonstrate in the particular case that such consideration is required to avoid an unsafe and unsound business practice; or

2. Race, color, religion, sex, marital status, national origin or ancestry.

It is illegal to consider the racial, ethnic, religious or national origin composition of a neighborhood or geographic area surrounding a housing accommodation or whether or not such composition is undergoing change, or is expected to undergo change, in appraising a housing accommodation or in determining whether or not, or under what terms and conditions, to provide financial assistance.

These provisions govern financial assistance for the purpose of the purchase, construction, rehabilitation or refinancing of a one-to-four unit family residence occupied by the owner and for the purpose of the home improvement of any one-to-four unit family residence.

If you have any questions about your rights, or if you wish to file a complaint, contact the management of this financial institution or the agency noted below:

I/we received a copy of this notice.

_____   _____
SAMPLE ONLY BORROWER, MR   Date   Date

LOAN APPLICATION

Uniform Residential Loan Application

This application is designed to be completed by the applicant(s) with the lender's assistance. Applicants should complete this form as "Borrower" or "Co-Borrower", as applicable. Co-Borrower information must also be provided (and the appropriate box checked) when ☐ the income or assets of a person other than the "Borrower" (including the Borrower's spouse) will be used as a basis for loan qualification or ☐ the income or assets of the Borrower's spouse will not be used as a basis for loan qualification, but his or her liabilities must be considered because the Borrower resides in a community property state, the security property is located in a community property state, or the Borrower is relying on other property located in a community property state as a basis for repayment of the loan.

I. TYPE OF MORTGAGE AND TERMS OF LOAN

Mortgage Applied for: ☐ VA ☒ Conventional (circled) ☐ Other
☐ FHA ☐ (circled)

Amount: $195,200
Interest Rate: 6.75%
No. of Months: 360
Amortization Type: ☒ Fixed Rate (circled) ☐ GPM ☐ ARM ☐ Other

II. PROPERTY INFORMATION AND PURPOSE OF LOAN

Subject Property Address: **1 MY NEW HOME - MY CITY - MY STATE 60000** (circled)

Legal Description: See title

No. of Units: 1 (circled)
Year Built: 2008

Purpose of Loan: ☒ Purchase (circled) ☐ Refinance ☐ Construction ☐ Construction-Permanent ☐ Other

Property will be: ☒ Primary Residence (circled) ☐ Secondary Residence ☐ Investment

Title will be held in what Name(s): **MR Borrower**

Estate will be held in: ☒ Fee Simple ☐ Leasehold

III. BORROWER INFORMATION

IV. EMPLOYMENT INFORMATION

Page 1 of 4

V. Monthly Income and Combined Housing Expensive Information

Gross Monthly Income	Borrower	Co-Borrower	Total	Combined Monthly Housing Expense	Present	Proposed
Base Empl. Income	$ 3,000.00	$	$ 3,000.00	Rent	500.00	
Overtime				First Mortgage (P&I)		853.29
Bonuses	500.00		500.00	Other Financing (P&I)		
Commissions	2,000.00		2,000.00	Hazard Insurance		40.00
Dividends/Interest				Real Estate Taxes		197.00
Net Rental Income				Mortgage Insurance		
Other				Homeowner Assn. Dues		
				Other:		
Total	$ 5,500.00	$	$ 5,500.00	Total	$ 500.00	1,090.29

Self Employed Borrower(s) may be required to provide additional documentation such as tax returns and financial statements.

Describe Other Income — Notice: Alimony, child support, or separate maintenance income need not be revealed if the Borrower (B) or Co-Borrower (C) does not choose to have it considered for repaying this loan.

B/C		Monthly Amount
		$

VI. Assets and Liabilities

This Statement and any applicable supporting schedules may be completed jointly by both married and unmarried Co-borrowers if their assets and liabilities are sufficiently joined so that the Statement can be meaningfully and fairly presented on a combined basis; otherwise, separate Statements and Schedules are required. If the Co-Borrower section was completed about a spouse, this Statement and supporting schedules must be completed about that spouse also.

Completed ☐ Jointly ☒ Not Jointly

ASSETS Description	Cash or Market Value	Liabilities and Pledged Assets. List the creditor's name, address and account number for all outstanding debts, including automobile loans, revolving charge accounts, real estate loans, alimony, child support, stock pledges, etc. Use continuation sheet, if necessary. Indicate by (*) those liabilities which will be satisfied upon sale of real estate owned or upon refinancing of the subject property.		
Cash deposit toward purchase held by: EARNEST	1,000			
		LIABILITIES	Monthly Payment & Months Left to Pay	Unpaid Balance
List checking and savings accounts below Name and address of Bank, S&L, or Credit Union TCK SAVINGS 111 JOHN NY 00000		Name and address of Company MASTERCARD 111 COLLECTION ST NY 00000	$ Payment/Months	
Acct. no. 111111	$ 15,000	Acct. no. 000000000	115 /8	800
Name and address of Bank, S&L, or Credit Union		Name and address of Company	$ Payment/Months	$
Acct. no.	$	Acct. no.		
Name and address of Bank, S&L, or Credit Union		Name and address of Company	$ Payment/Months	$
Acct. no.	$	Acct. no.		
Name and address of Bank, S&L, or Credit Union		Name and address of Company	$ Payment/Months	$
Acct. no.	$	Acct. no.		
Stocks & Bonds (Company name/ number & description) 401K IRA	90,000 2,000	Name and address of Company	$ Payment/Months	$
		Acct. no.		
Life insurance net cash value Face amount $	$	Name and address of Company	$ Payment/Months	$
Subtotal Liquid Assets	$ 108,000			
Real estate owned (enter market value from schedule of real estate owned)	$	Acct. no. Name and address of Company	$ Payment/Months	$
Vested interest in retirement fund	$			
Net worth of business(es) owned (attach financial statement)	$			
Automobiles owned (make and year) VOLKSWAGON	15,000	Acct. no. Alimony/Child Support/Separate Maintenance Payments Owed to:	$	
Other Assets (itemize) BOAT	12,000	Job Related Expense (child care, union dues, etc.)	$	
		Total Monthly Payments	$ 125	
Total Assets a.	$ 135,000	Net Worth (a minus b) ⇒ $ 134,200	Total Liabilities b.	$ 800

VI Assets and Liabilities (con't)

Schedule of Real Estate Owned (if additional properties are owned, use continuation sheet)

Property Address (enter S if sold, PS if pending sale or R if rental being held for income)	Type of Property	Present Market Value	Amount of Mortgages & Liens	Gross Rental Income	Mortgage Payments	Insurance, Maintenance, Taxes & Misc.	Net Rental Income
		$	$	$	$	$	$
Totals		$	$	$	$	$	$

List any additional names under which credit has previously been received and indicate appropriate creditor name(s) and account number(s):

Alternate Name	Creditor Name	Account Number

VII Details of Transaction

a. Purchase price	$ 150,000.00
b. Alterations, improvements, repairs	
c. Land (if acquired separately)	
d. Refinance (incl. debts to be paid off)	
e. Estimated prepaid items	839.63
f. Estimated closing costs	3,722.00
g. PMI, MIP, Funding Fee	
h. Discount (if Borrower will pay)	
i. Total costs (add items a through h)	154,561.63
j. Subordinate financing	
k. Borrower's closing costs paid by Seller	
l. Other Credits (explain) Cash Deposit	1,000.00
m. Loan amount (exclude PMI, MIP, Funding Fee financed)	135,000.00
n. PMI, MIP, Funding Fee financed	
o. Loan amount (add m & n)	135,000.00
p. Cash from/to Borrower (subtract j, k, l & o from i)	18,561.63

VIII Declarations

If you answer "yes" to any questions a through i, please use continuation sheet for explanation.

	Borrower	Co-Borrower
	Yes No	Yes No
a. Are there any outstanding judgments against you?	☐ ☒	☐ ☐
b. Have you been declared bankrupt within the past 7 years?	☐ ☒	☐ ☐
c. Have you had property foreclosed upon or given title or deed in lieu thereof in the last 7 years?	☐ ☒	☐ ☐
d. Are you a party to a lawsuit?	☐ ☒	☐ ☐
e. Have you directly or indirectly been obligated on any loan which resulted in foreclosure, transfer of title in lieu of foreclosure, or judgment?	☐ ☒	☐ ☐
f. Are you presently delinquent or in default on any Federal debt or any other loan, mortgage, financial obligation, bond, or loan guarantee?	☐ ☒	☐ ☐
g. Are you obligated to pay alimony, child support, or separate maintenance?	☐ ☒	☐ ☐
h. Is any part of the down payment borrowed?	☐ ☒	☐ ☐
i. Are you a co-maker or endorser on a note?	☐ ☒	☐ ☐
j. Are you a U.S. citizen?	☒ ☐	☐ ☐
k. Are you a permanent resident alien?	☐ ☒	☐ ☐
l. Do you intend to occupy the property as your primary residence? If "Yes," complete question m below.	☒ ☐	☐ ☐
m. Have you had an ownership interest in a property in the last three years?	☐ ☒	☐ ☐
(1) What type of property did you own—principal residence (PR), second home (SH), or investment property (IP)?		
(2) How did you hold title to the home—solely by yourself (S), jointly with your spouse (SP), or jointly with another person (O)?		

IX Acknowledgement and Agreement

[Acknowledgement and agreement text]

Borrower's Signature: X _____ Date _____
Co-Borrower's Signature: X _____ Date _____

X Information for Government monitoring purposes

The following information is requested by the Federal Government for certain types of loans related to a dwelling in order to monitor the lender's compliance with equal credit opportunity, fair housing and home mortgage disclosure laws. You are not required to furnish this information, but are encouraged to do so. The law provides that a Lender may not discriminate neither on the basis of this information, nor on whether you choose to furnish it. If you furnish this information, please provide both ethnicity and race. For race, you may check more than one designation. If you do not furnish ethnicity, race, or sex, under Federal regulations, this lender is required to note the information on the basis of visual observation or surname. If you do not wish to furnish the information, please check the box below. (Lender must review the above material to assure that the disclosures satisfy all requirements to which the lender is subject under applicable state law for the particular type of loan applied for.)

BORROWER ☐ I do not wish to furnish this information
CO-BORROWER ☐ I do not wish to furnish this information

Ethnicity:	☐ Hispanic or Latino ☐ Not Hispanic or Latino	Ethnicity:	☐ Hispanic or Latino ☐ Not Hispanic or Latino
Race:	☐ American Indian or Alaska Native ☐ Asian ☒ Black or African American ☐ Native Hawaiian or Other Pacific Islander ☐ White	Race:	☐ American Indian or Alaska Native ☐ Asian ☐ Black or African American ☐ Native Hawaiian or Other Pacific Islander ☐ White
Sex:	☐ Female ☒ Male	Sex:	☐ Female ☐ Male

To be Completed by Interviewer
This application was taken by:
☒ Face-to-face Interview
☐ Mail
☐ Telephone
☐ Internet

Interviewer's Name (print or type): BETTY
Interviewer's Signature: _____ Date _____
Interviewer's Phone Number (incl. area code): 000-000-0000

Name and Address of Interviewer's Employer:
YOUR LENDING CO
111 JOHN ST.
BLOOMINGTON, NY 111111
(P) 111-111-11111

Continuation Sheet/Residential Loan Application

Use this continuation sheet if you need more space to complete the Residential Loan Application. Mark B for Borrower or C for Co-Borrower	Borrower:	Agency Case Number:
	Co-Borrower:	Lender Case Number:

I/We fully understand that it is a Federal crime punishable by fine or imprisonment, or both, to knowingly make any false statements concerning any of the above facts as applicable under the provisions of Title 18, United States Code, Section 1001, et seq.

Borrower's Signature	Date	Co-Borrower's Signature	Date
X		X	

REQUIRED DOCUMENTATION

In order to process your loan request we will require the following documentation

INCOME
- Most recent pay stubs for 1 month
- Last 2 year's W-2 forms
- 2 year's signed individual federal tax returns including all schedules
- Last 2 year's corporate tax returns
- Last 2 year's partnership returns
- Year to date profit and loss statement
- Copy of employers relocation/transfer policy
- Lease agreement-all rental units, 12 months history of receipt of alimony, child support or maintenance if this will be used for income qualification purpose
- K1's for the year (2) _____ for _____

ASSETS
- Copy of canceled earnest money checks
- Name, address and current account numbers for all checking and savings.
- Last 3 months bank statements for all accounts
- Gift letter
- Source of gift funds statement
- Social Security awards letter
- Pension award letter

NEW PURCHASE
- Fully executed purchase contract and all riders
- Name and address and phone number of your attorney and Realtor
- Sold contract/listing agreement
- Condo Association articles and bylaws

MORTGAGE REFINANCE
- Update survey no older than 3 months

- Homeowners insurance policy with agents name and phone number
- Title policy or legal application
- Well Test
- Septic Test

OTHER
- Condo name, address and phone number
- Letter from Condo Association starting monthly assessment is up to date
- Certify copy of death certificate
- _____
- _____
- _____
- _____

DEBTS/OBLIGATIONS
- Name, address and account numbers for each mortgage or installment loan
- Account numbers for open revolving credit
- Certified copy of divorce decree
- Landlord name and address
- Last 12 months canceled checks (front and back) for _____
- Proof of credit union deduction on _____ pay stubs-is this a loan or savings account (could be proved via credit union statement)
- Bankruptcy discharge and list of creditors
- Most recent credit union statement for
- Year _____ End _____ statement
- Letter of explanation for _____

nal items may be requested at a later time.)

HUD/VA Addendum to Uniform Residential Loan Application

Part I - Identifying Information (mark the type of application)

1. ☐ VA Application for Home Loan Guaranty ☐ HUD/FHA Application for Insurance under the National Housing Act
2. Agency Case No: (include any suffix)
3. Lender's Case Number:
4. Section of the Act (for HUD case)
5. Borrower's Name & Present Address (include zip code)
6. Property Address (including name of subdivision, lot & block no. & zip code)
7. Loan Amount (include the UFMIP if for HUD or Funding Fee if for V.A.) $
8. Interest Rate: %
9. Proposed Maturity: yrs. mos.
10. Discount Amt.: (only if borrower is permitted to pay) $
11. Amount of Up Front Premium: $
12a. Amount of Monthly Premium: /mo.
12b. Term of Monthly Premium: months
13. Lender's I.D. Code:
14. Sponsor/Agent I.D. Code:
15. Lender's Name & Address (include zip code)
16. Name & Address of Sponsor/Agent:

Type or Print all entries clearly

17. Lender's Telephone Number

V.A.: The veteran and the lender hereby apply to the Secretary of Veterans Affairs for Guaranty of the loan described here under Section 3710, Chapter 37, Title 38, United States Code, to the full extent permitted by the veteran's entitlement and severally agree that the Regulations promulgated pursuant to Chapter 37, and in effect on the date of the loan shall govern the rights, duties, and liabilities of the parties.

18. First Time Homebuyer?
a. ☐ Yes
b. ☐ No

19. V.A. Only: Title will be Vested in:
☐ Veteran
☐ Veteran & Spouse
☐ Other (Specify):

20. Purpose of Loan (blocks 9 - 12 are for V.A. loans only)
1) ☐ Purchase Existing Home Previously Occupied
2) ☐ Finance Improvements to Existing Property
3) ☐ Refinance (Refi.)
4) ☐ Purchase New Condo. Unit
5) ☐ Purchase Existing Condo. Unit
6) ☐ Purchase Existing Home Not Previously Occupied
7) ☐ Construct Home (proceeds to be paid out during construction)
8) ☐ Finance Co-op Purchase
9) ☐ Purchase Permanently Sited Manufactured Home
10) ☐ Purchase Permanently Sited Manufactured Home & Lot
11) ☐ Refi. Permanently Sited Manufactured Home to Buy Lot
12) ☐ Refi. Permanently Sited Manufactured Home/Lot Loan

Part II - Lender's Certification

21. The undersigned lender makes the following certifications to induce the Department of Veterans Affairs to issue a certificate of commitment to guarantee the subject loan or a Loan Guaranty Certificate under Title 38, U.S. code, or to induce the Department of Housing and Urban Development - Federal Housing Commissioner to issue a firm commitment for mortgage insurance or a Mortgage Insurance Certificate under the National Housing Act.

A. The loan terms furnished in the Uniform Residential Loan Application and this Addendum are true, accurate and complete.
B. The information contained in the Uniform Residential Loan Application and this Addendum was obtained directly from the borrower by a full-time employee of the undersigned lender or its duly authorized agent and is true to the best of the lender's knowledge and belief.
C. The credit report submitted on the subject borrower (and co-borrower, if any) was ordered by the undersigned lender or its duly authorized agent directly from the credit bureau which prepared the report and was received directly from said credit bureau.
D. The verification of employment and verification of deposits were requested and received by the lender or its duly authorized agent without passing through the hands of any third persons and are true to the best of the lender's knowledge and belief.
E. The Uniform Residential Loan Application and this Addendum were signed by the borrower after all sections were completed.
F. This proposed loan to the named borrower meets the income and credit requirements of the governing law in the judgment of the undersigned.
G. To the best of my knowledge and belief, I and my firm and its principals: (1) are not presently debarred, suspended, proposed for debarment, declared ineligible, or voluntarily excluded from covered transactions by any Federal department or agency; (2) have not, within a three-year period preceding this proposal, been convicted of or had a civil judgment rendered against them for (a) commission of fraud or a criminal offense in connection with obtaining, attempting to obtain, or performing a public (Federal, State or local) transaction or contract under a public transaction; (b) violation of Federal or State antitrust statutes or commission of embezzlement, theft, forgery, bribery, falsification or destruction of records, making false statements, or receiving stolen property; (3) are not presently indicted for or otherwise criminally or civilly charged by a governmental entity (Federal, State or local) with commission of any of the offenses enumerated in paragraph G(2) of this certification; and (4) have not, within a three-year period preceding this application/proposal, had one or more public transactions (Federal, State or local) terminated for cause or default.

Items "H" through "J" are to be completed as applicable for V.A. loans only.
H. The names and functions of any duly authorized agents who developed on behalf of the lender any of the information or supporting credit data submitted are as follows:

Name & Address:	Function: (e.g. obtained information on the Uniform Residential Loan Application, ordered credit report, verifications of employment, deposits, etc.)

If no agent is shown above, the undersigned lender affirmatively certifies that all information and supporting credit data were obtained directly by the lender.

I. The undersigned lender understands and agrees that it is responsible for the omissions, errors, or acts of agents identified in item H as to the functions with which they are identified
J. The proposed loan conforms otherwise with the applicable provisions of Title 38, U.S. Code, and of the regulations concerning guaranty or insurance of loans to veterans.

Signature of Officer of Lender	Title of Officer of Lender	Date(mm/dd/yyyy)
X		

V.A. Form 26-1802a (3/98)

Part III - Notices to Borrowers Public Reporting Burden for this collection of information is estimated to average 6 minutes per response, including the time for reviewing instructions, searching existing data sources, gathering and maintaining the data needed, and completing and reviewing the collection of information. This agency may not conduct or sponsor, and a person is not required to respond to, a collection information unless that collection displays a valid OMB Control Number.

Privacy Act Information The information requested on the Uniform Residential Loan Application and this Addendum is authorized by 38 U.S.C. 3710 (if for DVA) and 12 U.S.C. 1701 et seq. (if for HUD/FHA). The Debt Collection Act of 1982, Pub. Law 97-365, and HUD's Housing and Community Development Act of 1987, 42 U.S.C. 3543, require persons applying for a federally insured or guaranteed loan to furnish his/her social security number(SSN). You must provide all the requested information, including your SSN. HUD and/or V.A. may conduct a computer match to verify the information you provide. HUD and/or V.A. may disclose certain information to Federal, State and local agencies when relevant to civil, criminal, or regulatory investigations and prosecutions. It will not otherwise be disclosed or released outside of HUD or V.A., except as required and permitted by law. The information will be used to determine whether you qualify as a mortgagor. Any disclosure of information outside V.A. or HUD/FHA will be made only as permitted by law. Failure to provide any of the requested information, including SSN, may result in disapproval of your loan application. This notice to you is required by the Right to Financial Privacy Act of 1978 that V.A. or HUD/FHA has a right of access to financial records held by financial institutions in connection with the consideration or administration of assistance to you. Financial records involving your transaction will be available to V.A. and HUD/FHA without further notice or authorization but will not be disclosed or released by this institution to another Government Agency or Department without your consent except as required or permitted by law.

Caution Delinquencies, defaults, foreclosures and abuses of mortgage loans involving programs of the Federal Government can be costly and detrimental to your credit, now and in the future. The lender in this transaction, its agents and assigns as well as the Federal Government, its agencies, agents and assigns, are authorized to take any and all of the following actions in the event loan payments become delinquent on the mortgage loan described in the attached application: (1) Report your name and account information to a credit bureau; (2) Assess additional interest and penalty charges for the period of time that payment is not made; (3) Assess charges to cover additional administrative costs incurred by the Government to service your account; (4) Offset amounts owed to you under other Federal programs; (5) Refer your account to a private attorney, collection agency or mortgage servicing agency to collect the amount due, foreclose the mortgage, sell the property and seek judgment against you for any deficiency; (6) Refer your account to the Department of Justice for litigation in the courts; (7) If you are a current or retired Federal employee, take action to offset your salary, or civil service retirement benefits; (8) Refer your debt to the Internal Revenue Service for offset against any amount owed to you as an income tax refund; and (9) Report any resulting written-off debt of yours to the Internal Revenue Service as your taxable income. All of these actions can and will be used to recover any debts owed when it is determined to be in the interest of the lender and/or the Federal Government to do so.

Part IV - Borrower Certification

22. Complete the following for a HUD/FHA Mortgage

22 a. Do you own or have you sold other real estate within the past 60 months on which there was a HUD / FHA mortgage? ☐ Yes ☐ No

Is it to be sold? ☐ Yes ☐ No

22 b. Sales Price $

22 c. Original Mortgage Amount $

22 d. Address:

22 e. If the dwelling to be covered by this mortgage is to be rented, is it a part of, adjacent or contiguous to any project subdivision or group of concentrated rental properties involving eight or more dwelling units in which you have any financial interest? ☐ Yes ☐ No If "Yes" give details.

22 f. Do you own more than four dwellings? ☐ Yes ☐ No If "Yes" submit form HUD-92561

23. Complete for V.A. - Guaranteed Mortgage. Have you ever had a V.A. home loan? ☐ Yes ☐ No

24. Applicable for Both V.A. & HUD. As a home loan borrower, you will be legally obligated to make the mortgage payments called for by your mortgage loan contract. The fact that you dispose of your property after the loan has been made will not relieve you of liability for making these payments. Payment of the loan in full is ordinarily the way liability on a mortgage note is ended. Some home buyers have the mistaken impression that if they sell their homes when they move to another locality, or dispose of it for any other reasons, they are no longer liable for the mortgage payments and that liability for these payments is solely that of the new owners. Even though the new owners may agree in writing to assume liability for your mortgage payments, this assumption agreement will not relieve you from liability to the holder of the note which you signed when you obtained the loan to buy the property. Unless you are able to sell the property to a buyer who is acceptable to V.A. or to HUD/FHA and who will assume the payment of your obligation to the lender, you will not be relieved from liability to repay any claim which V.A. or HUD/FHA may be required to pay your lender on account of default in your loan payments. The amount of any such claim payment will be a debt owed by you to the Federal Government. This debt will be the object of established collection procedures.

25. I, the Undersigned Borrower(s) Certify that:

(1) I have read and understand the foregoing concerning my liability on the loan and Part III Notices to Borrowers.

(2) Occupancy: (for V.A. only - mark the applicable box)

☐ (a) I now actually occupy the above-described property as my home or intend to move into and occupy said property as my home within a reasonable period of time or intend to reoccupy it after the completion of major alterations, repairs or improvements.

☐ (b) My spouse is on active military duty and in his or her absence, I occupy or intend to occupy the property securing this loan as my home.

☐ (c) I previously occupied the property securing this loan as my home. (for interest rate reductions)

☐ (d) While my spouse was on active military duty and unable to occupy the property securing this loan, I previously occupied the property that is securing this loan as my home. (for interest rate reduction loans)

Note: If box 2b or 2d is checked, the veteran's spouse must also sign below.

(3) Mark the applicable box (not applicable for Home Improvement or Refinancing Loan) I have been informed that ($_____) is:

☐ the reasonable value of the property as determined by V.A. or;

☐ the statement of appraised value as determined by HUD/FHA.

Note: If the contract price or cost exceeds the V.A. "Reasonable Value" or HUD/FHA "Statement of Appraised Value," mark either item (a) or item (b), whichever is applicable.

☐ (a) I was aware of this valuation when I signed my contract and I have paid or will pay in cash from my own resources at or prior to loan closing a sum equal to the difference between the contract purchase price or cost and the V.A. or HUD/FHA established value. I do not and will not have outstanding after loan closing any unpaid contractual obligation on account of such cash payment.

☐ (b) I was not aware of this valuation when I signed my contract but have elected to complete the transaction at the contract purchase price or cost. I have paid or will pay in cash from my own resources at or prior to loan closing a sum equal to the difference between contract purchase price or cost and the V.A. or HUD/FHA established value. I do not and will not have outstanding after loan closing any unpaid contractual obligation on account of such cash payment.

(4) Neither I, nor anyone authorized to act for me, will refuse to sell or rent, after the making of a bona fide offer, or refuse to negotiate for the sale or rental of, or otherwise make unavailable or deny the dwelling or property covered by his/her loan to any person because of race, color, religion, sex, handicap, familial status or national origin. I recognize that any restrictive covenant on this property relating to race, color, religion, sex, handicap, familial status or national origin is illegal and void and civil action for preventive relief may be brought by the Attorney General of the United States in any appropriate U.S. District Court against any person responsible for the violation of the applicable law.

(5) All information in this application is given for the purpose of obtaining a loan to be insured under the National Housing Act or guaranteed by the Department of Veterans Affairs and the information in the Uniform Residential Loan Application and this Addendum is true and complete to the best of my knowledge and belief. Verification may be obtained from any source named herein.

(6) For HUD Only (for properties constructed prior to 1978) I have received information on lead paint poisoning. ☐ Yes ☐ Not Applicable

(7) I am aware that neither HUD/FHA nor V.A. warrants the condition or value of the property.

Signature(s) of Borrower(s) - Do not sign unless this application is fully completed. Read the certifications carefully & review accuracy of this application

Date:

X

Federal statutes provide severe penalties for any fraud, intentional misrepresentation, or criminal connivance or conspiracy purpose to influence the issuance of any guaranty or insurance by the VA Secretary or the HUD/FHA commissioner.

V.A. Form 26-1802a (3/98)

Direct Endorsement Approval for a HUD/FHA Insured Mortgage

Part I - Identifying Information (mark the type of application)

1. ☐ HUD/FHA Application for Insurance under the National Housing Act

2. Agency Case No: (include any suffix)
3. Lender's Case Number:
4. Section of the Act (for HUD cases)

5. Borrower's Name & Present Address (include zip code)

7. Loan Amount (include the UFMIP): $
8. Interest Rate: %
9. Proposed Maturity: yrs. mos.

6. Property Address (including name of subdivision, lot & block no. & zip code):

10. Discount Amt.: (only if borrower is permitted to pay) $
11. Amount of Up Front Premium: $
12a. Amount of Monthly Premium: $ /mo.
12b. Term of Monthly Premium: month

13. Lender's I.D. Code:
14. Sponsor/Agent I.D. Code:

15. Lender's Name & Address (include zip code)

16. Name & Address of Sponsor/Agent:

Type or Print all entries clearly

17. Lender's Telephone Number:

☐ **Approved:** Approved subject to the additional conditions stated below, if any.

Date Mortgage Approved _____ Date Approval Expires _____

☐ **Modified & Approved as follows:**

| Loan Amount (include UFMIP) | Interest Rate: % | Proposed Maturity: yrs. mos. | Monthly Payment: $ | Amount of Up Front Premium: $ | Amount of Monthly Premium: $ | Term of Monthly Premium: months |

Additional Conditions:

☐ If this is proposed construction, the builder has certified compliance with HUD requirements on form HUD-92541.
☐ If this is new construction, the lender certifies that the property is 100% complete (both on site and off site improvements) **and** the property meets HUD's minimum property standards.
☐ Form HUD-92544, Builder's Warranty is required.
☐ The property has a 10-year warranty.
☐ The property is to be insured under Section 221 (d)(2); a code compliance inspection is required.
☐ Owner-Occupancy Not required (item (b) of the Borrower's Certificate does not apply)
☐ The mortgage is a high loan-to-value ratio for non-occupant mortgagor in military.
☐ Other: (specify)

☐ This mortgage was rated as an "accept" or "approve" by a FHA-approved automated underwriting system. As such, the undersigned representative of the mortgagee certifies to the integrity of the data supplied by the lender used to determine the quality of the loan, that a Direct Endorsement Underwriter reviewed the appraisal (if applicable) and further certifies that this mortgage is eligible for HUD mortgage insurance under the Direct Endorsement program. I hereby make all certifications required for this mortgage as set forth in HUD Handbook 4000.4

Mortgagee Representative: _____

FHA-Approved Automated Underwriting System: _____

☐ This mortgage was rated as "refer" of "caution" by a FHA-approved automated underwriting system, and/or was manually underwritten by a Direct Endorsement underwriter. As such, the undersigned Direct Endorsement underwriter certifies that I have personally reviewed the appraisal report (if applicable), credit application, and all associated documents and have used due diligence in underwriting this mortgage. I find that this mortgage is eligible for HUD mortgage insurance under the Direct Endorsement program and I hereby make all certifications required for this mortgage as set forth in HUD Handbook 4000.4

Direct Endorsement Underwriter _____ DE's CHUMS ID Number _____

FHA-Approved AUS (if appropriate) _____

The Mortgagee, it's owners, officers or directors ☐ do ☐ do not have a financial interest in or a relationship, by affiliation or ownership, with the builder or seller involved in this transaction.

Borrower's Certification & Authorization

Certification

The undersigned certify the following:

1. I/We have applied for a mortgage loan Sample Mortgage company.. In applying for the loan, I/We completed a loan application containing various information on the purpose of the loan, the amount and source of the down payment, employment and income information, and assets and liabilities. I/We made no misrepresentation in the loan application or other documents, nor did I/We omit any pertinent information.
2. I/We understand and agree that Sample Mortgage co. may sell my/our mortgage loan review process to a full documentation program. This may include verifying the information provided on the application with the employer and/or the financial institution.
3. I/We fully understand that it is a Federal crime punishable by fine or imprisonment, or both, to knowingly make any false statements when applying for this mortgage, as applicable under the provisions of Title 18, United States Code, Section 1014.

Authorization to Release Information

1. I/We have applied for a mortgage loan from Sample Mortgage company.. As part f the application process, Sample Mortgage company. and the mortgage guaranty insurer (if any), may verify information contained in my/our loan application and in other documents required in connection with the loan, either before the loan is closed or as part of its quality control program, and such information is subject to re-verification after the date of the loan.
2. I/We authorize you to provide the Sample Mortgage company., and any investor to whom Sample Mortgage company. may sell my mortgage, and to the mortgage guaranty (if any), any and all information and documentation that they request. Such information includes, but is not limited to, employment history and income: bank, money, money market, and similar account balances; credit history; copies of income tax returns; and rental/mortgage verification.
3. Sample Mortgage company. or any investor that purchases the mortgage, guaranty insurer (if any), may address this authorization to any party named in the loan application.
4. A copy of this authorization may be accepted as an original.
5. You prompt reply to Sample Mortgage company., the investor that purchased the mortgage, or the mortgage guaranty insurer (if any) is appreciated.

Equal Credit Opportunity Act

The Equal Credit Opportunity Act prohibits creditors from discriminating against credit applicants on the basis of race, color, religion, national origin, sex, marital status, age (provided that the applicant has the capacity to enter into a binding contract), because all or part of the applicants income is derived from a public assistance program, or because the applicant has in good faith exercised any right under the Consumer Credit Protection Act. The Federal Agency that administers compliance with this law concerning this creditor is the Federal Commission, Equal Credit Opportunity, Washington, D. D. 20590.

Borrower   Co-Borrower

_____   _____
Printed Name   Printed Name

_____   ___   _____   ___
Signature   Date   Signature   Date

Your Mortgage company. Representative

Borrower Signature Authorization

Privacy Act Notice: This information is to be used by the agency collecting it or its assignees in determining whether you qualify as a prospective mortgagor under its program. It will not be disclosed outside the agency except as required and permitted by law. You do not have to provide this information, but if you do not your application for approval as a prospective mortgagor or borrower may be delayed or rejected. The information requested in this form is authorized by Title 38, USC, Chapter 37 (if VA); by 12 USC, Section 1701 et. seq. (if HUD/FHA); by 42 USC, Section 1452b (if HUD/CPD) ; and Title 42 USC, 1471 et. seq., or 7 USC, 1921 et. seq. (if USDA/FmHA).

Part I - General Information

1. Borrower(s)	2. Name and address of Lender/Broker
	Frontier Bank, FSB PO Box 981180 Park City, UT 84098-1180 TEL: 435-615-2265 FAX: 435-615-2278
3. Date	4. Loan Number	

Part II - Borrower Authorization

I hereby authorize the Lender/Broker to verify my past and present employment earnings records, bank accounts, stock holdings, and any other asset balances that are needed to process my mortgage loan application. I further authorize the Lender/Broker to order a consumer credit report and verify other credit information, including past and present mortgage and landlord references. It is understood that a copy of this form will also serve as authorization.

The information the Lender/Broker obtains is only to be used in the processing of my application for a mortgage loan.

_____ _____
Borrower   Date

_____ _____
Borrower   Date

Understanding The Loan Application

Step-by-Step

Line by Line
Break Down

**Print or view clear copy
Freddie Mac form 1003**

The FNMA1003/FHLMC 65 Residential Loan Application is composed often sections (pages 1-3) and a continuation sheet (page 4).

Page 1: Requests information on the loan amount and type, purpose of the loan, borrowers residence and employment history.

I Type of mortgage and terms of loan
II Property information and purpose of loan
III Borrower Information
IV Employment Information

Page 2: The financial portion of the application i.e. monthly income, housing expense information and personal financial statement.

V Monthly income and combined housing expense information
VI Assets and liabilities

Page 3: Addresses of present real estate owned, details of the proposed transaction, declarations, acknowledgment agreement and monitoring information.

VII Details of transaction
VIII Declarations
IX Acknowledgments and agreements
X Information for Gov. monitoring purpose

Page 4: Continuation Page: to be used if more space is needed to Complete the portions of the application.
Mark (b) for borrower or Mark(c) co-borrower

Completing the application becomes child's play after reading this section and the step-by-step, line by line instructions.

Important Tip
When taking the 1003 application, always remember that it must be complete with no short cuts. A clean, complete application leads to solid loan package.

Note: The states, Ohio, South Carolina, Main, and Massachusetts have special requirements for the 1003/65 applications. Always check with your state for clarification.

Section 1 Types of Mortgages and Terms of Loans

1. Check the appropriate box, either co-borrower or community property state.
For single borrowers leave this blank. (Above the section in the paragraph)
2. Check the appropriate box for type of mortgage required. VA, FHA, Conventional, FMHA or other.
3. Agency Case Number. Used by your company for internal processing, so be sure to ask your boss or manager.

4. Lender case Number Same as 3.
5. Amount. The loan amount must be shown and should be rounded to the next highest $100 increment.
6. Interest rates should be expressed as a decimal to three places. Example: 7.375
7. The term of the loan should be shown in months, not in years for example: 180 (15 years) ; 240 (20 years) ; 300 (25 years) ; 360 (30 yrs)
8. Check the appropriate box for the type of amortization - fixed rate, graduated payments, adjustable rate or other (requires explanation)

Review and Check
Part 2 PROPERTY INFORMATION AND PURPOSE OF LOAN

√ Check for all this information on Loan Application

Subject Property Address: Complete (Street, City, State, Zip) * Note: P.O. Box Not acceptable
On Contract and always on the Appraisal
NO. of Units: Typically 1 but not limit to Example (Single family, Duplex, Triplex, etc.)
Year Built- Example 1999 but see Sales Contract or Appraisal for accuracy
Purpose of Loan- Example Purchase: Loan is for the purchase of the existing property
Sometimes new Construction, Refinance or other (Refer to Contract, Loan Officer or Appraisal)
For the purpose of Refinance, New Construction or other use the later area
*Refinance refer to their old Hud 1 form (original purchase of existing home) for information
Title to be held in what Name(s) : Example
Mr. First Borrower or Mr. First Borrower and Mrs. Lady Borrower

Joint Tenancy — give joint ownership by two or more persons not necessarily married giving equal rights and interest   ^
Source Of Down Payment, Settlement Charges

 Applicant should have adequate funds for down payment and settlement charges. These funds must be verifiable and have acceptable source. Example: Savings, Checking, Gift, Equity from previous sale.. See Loan Officer for Guidelines

Fee Simple: see above source

Borrower	III. BORROWER INFORMATION	Co-Borrower
Borrower's Name (Include Jr. or Sr. if applicable)		Co-Borrower's Name (Include Jr. or Sr. if applicable)

Social Security Number	Home Phone (incl. Area code)	DOB (mm/dd/yyyy)	Yrs. School	Social Security Number	Home Phone (incl. Area code)	DOB (mm/dd/yyyy)	Yrs. School

☐ Married ☐ Separated ☐ Unmarried (include single, divorced, widowed)	Dependents (not listed by Co-Borrower) no. ages	☐ Married ☐ Separated ☐ Unmarried (include single, divorced, widowed)	Dependents (not listed by Borrower) no. ages
Present Address (street, city, state, ZIP) ☐ Own ☐ Rent __No. Yrs.		Present Address (street, city, state, ZIP) ☐ Own ☐ Rent __No. Yrs.	
Mailing Address, if different from Present Address		Mailing Address, if different from Present Address	
If residing at present address for less than two years, complete the following:			
Former Address (street, city, state, ZIP) ☐ Own ☐ Rent __No. Yrs.		Former Address (street, city, state, ZIP) ☐ Own ☐ Rent __No. Yrs.	

Review and Check
Part 3 Borrower Information

√ Check for all this information on this Application
Subject Property Address: Complete (Street, City, State, Zip) * Note: P.O. Box Not acceptable On Contract and always on the Appraisal
Borrowers) Complete Legal Name including Jr. Sr. Example (Mr. First Borrower Jr.)
* MUST Complete with accuracy this section using all names that will be on die loan or title
Co-Borrower(s) Complete Legal Name if using Co-Borrower(s)
Borrowers) Social Security Number
This number is required to check Credit. It is also used to check Employment, Federal Tax returns and other vital information

Co-Borrower(s) Social Security Number
This number is required to check Credit. It is also used to check Employment, Federal Tax returns, and other vital information Example 1999 but see Sales Contract or Appraisal for accuracy
Borrower's Home Phone Number Current Home Phone Listing {Include area code)
Borrower's Age
Borrower's School (years attended)

*If less than 2 years also include Previous or former Address If Using C0-Borrower(s) make sure to include ALL of their complete and accurate information

Borrower	IV. EMPLOYMENT INFORMATION		Co-Borrower
Name & Address of Employer ☐ Self Employed	Yrs. on this job	Name & Address of Employer ☐ Self Employed	Yrs. on this job
	Yrs. employed in this line of work/profession		Yrs. employed in this line of work/profession
Position/Title/Type of Business	Business Phone (incl. area code)	Position/Title/Type of Business	Business Phone (incl. area code)

If employed in current position for less than two years or if currently employed in more than one position, complete the following:

Name & Address of Employer ☐ Self Employed	Dates (from - to)	Name & Address of Employer ☐ Self Employed	Dates (from - to)
	Monthly Income $		Monthly Income $
Position/Title/Type of Business	Business Phone (incl. area code)	Position/Title/Type of Business	Business Phone (incl. area code)
Name & Address of Employer ☐ Self Employed	Dates (from - to)	Name & Address of Employer ☐ Self Employed	Dates (from - to)
	Monthly Income $		Monthly Income $
Position/Title/Type of Business	Business Phone (incl. area code)	Position/Title/Type of Business	Business Phone (incl. area code)

Freddie Mac Form 65 7/05   Page 2 of 8   Fannie Mae Form 1003 7/05

(encircled: 4)

Part 4 √ Check for all this information on Loan Application

Name and Address of Employer- Complete (Street, City, State, Zip)

- Note: P.O. Box Not acceptable *Always Best to Verify Employment with Personnel of Payroll Dept.

Number of Years on the job Example (2 ½ or 2yrs 6mo) Number of Years employed in this line of work Example 6

Position/Title Example (Mortgage Loan Processor, Pilot, Waitress, etc.)
Business Phone Number

Self- Employed Box

This box checked if Borrower is self employed and will be required to furnish:
Two years of Federal Income Tax Returns, Business Returns etc.

Always refer to Conditions on Loan and the Loan Officer for further Details

If less than two years or more than one position

- Repeat the same information in box provide below

Repeat the same information for Co-Borrower(s) if applicable

Gross Monthly Income	Borrower	Co-Borrower	Total	Combined Monthly Housing Expense	Present	Proposed
Base Empl. Income	3,000.00		3,000.00	Rent	500.00	
Overtime				First Mortgage (P&I)		853.39
Bonuses	500.00		500.00	Other Financing (P&I)		
Commissions	2,000.00		2,000.00	Hazard Insurance		40.00
Dividends/Interest				Real Estate Taxes		197.00
Net Rental Income				Mortgage Insurance		
Other				Homeowner Assn. Dues		
				Other		
Total	5,500.00		5,500.00	Total	500.00	1,090.39

Review and check
Part 5 MONTHLY INCOME AND COMBINED HOUSING EXPENSE INFORMATION

√ Check for all this information on Loan Application

Gross Monthly Income Complete (Street, City, State, Zip)

*Note: P.O. Box Not acceptable

*The borrower and the Co-borrower's income is broken down separately and then totaled

Base Employee Income
Example (GROSS Monthly before Taxes, insurance, and other deductions)
Over Time (Monthly)
Bonuses (Any incentives, rewards or other income given by employee)
Commissions (Percentage of income from sales)
Dividend/Interest Income (Investment Statements for past 3 months, past two years of federal Tax Returns with a copy of the Schedule B Co confirm die Income)

Net Rental Income (Refer GO Section on Real Estate Owned) If applicable

Other type* of Income Received; Example (Child Support, alimony, Military or reserve pay, disability, or from a trust etc.) Total (Tally all above figures)
*FU1 in the appropriate amounts for second column

"Combined Monthly Housing Expense** Total (Tally all figures)

Review and check

Part 6 ASSETS AND LIABILITIES N Check for all this information on Loan Application

√ Check Small Print Box Jointly or Not Jointly (This box Mates that the co-borrower assets and liabilities should be shown jointly or separately)
- Cash Deposit Held by Example (Earnest Money/Check)
- Cash or Market Value (Earnest Check $1,000.00)
- List Checking and Savings accounts

List Complete and Accurate Name and Address of Financial Institution (s)
- Complete and Accurate Account Number (s)
- Amount or Amounts in Accounts

"   List All Stocks & Bonds with Company Example (401K, IRA, CD's, etc) (Name/account numbers) Amounts and description)
Life Insurance Rice Amount (Careful not to list or confuse Net Cash Value with Face)
SUBTOTAL LIQUID ASSETS

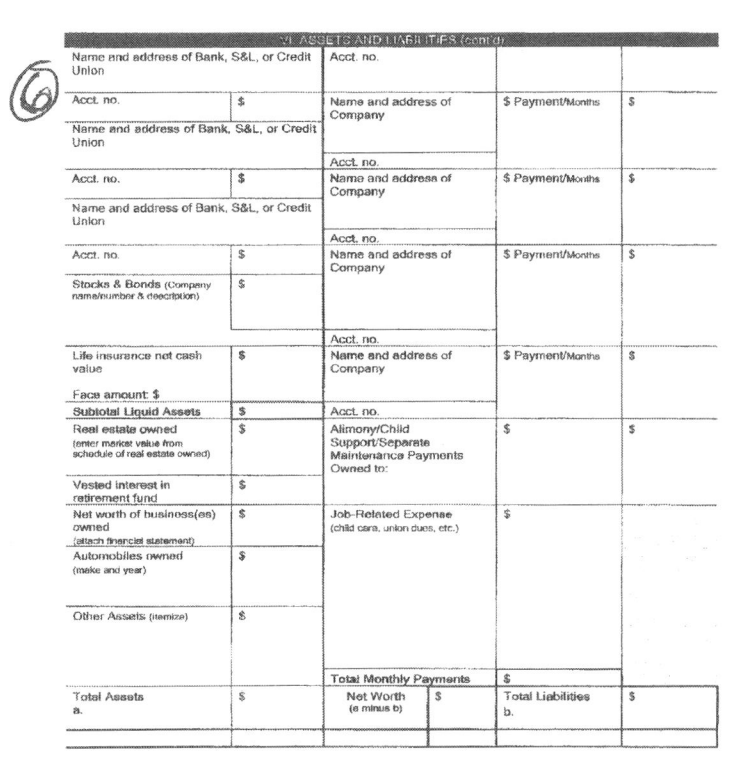

VI. ASSETS AND LIABILITIES (cont'd)					
Name and address of Bank, S&L, or Credit Union		Acct. no.			
Acct. no.	$	Name and address of Company		$ Payment/Months	$
Name and address of Bank, S&L, or Credit Union					
		Acct. no.			
Acct. no.	$	Name and address of Company		$ Payment/Months	$
Name and address of Bank, S&L, or Credit Union					
		Acct. no.			
Acct. no.	$	Name and address of Company		$ Payment/Months	$
Stocks & Bonds (Company name/number & description)	$				
		Acct. no.			
Life insurance net cash value Face amount: $	$	Name and address of Company		$ Payment/Months	$
Subtotal Liquid Assets	$	Acct. no.			
Real estate owned (enter market value from schedule of real estate owned)	$	Alimony/Child Support/Separate Maintenance Payments Owned to:		$	$
Vested interest in retirement fund	$				
Net worth of business(es) owned (attach financial statement)	$	Job-Related Expense (child care, union dues, etc.)		$	
Automobiles owned (make and year)	$				
Other Assets (itemize)	$				
		Total Monthly Payments		$	
Total Assets a.	$	Net Worth (a minus b)	$	Total Liabilities b.	$

Continuation of 6

- Real Estate Owned (Enter Market Value)
- Automobiles owned (make and Year)
- Net Worth of Business Owned (if an7- Self Employed)
- Other Assets (Furs, Boats, Coins, Notes etc.)
- Liabilities Names and Addresses of Companies must have
- Liabilities and Pledges (List all Credit, Charge Cards, Loins, etc.)
- You must have accurate account numbers for the credit report application.
- List monthly payments and unpaid balances on all debts. - If all debts do not fit on spaces provided use addendum page
- Alimony/Child Support/Separate Maintenance Payments owed to: - Supporting Documents may be required

- Job Related Expenses
- Government Loans Only, child care other job related
- Total Monthly Payments-   This is not the same as total liabilities
- Tally Payments ABOVE this Block –
- Net Worth (A Minus)
- After totaling all asset column (a) and die total Liabilities, column (b)

*Subtract b from a to get the total of Net Worth

Schedule of Real Estate Owned (If additional properties are owned, use continuation sheet.)

Property Address (enter S if sold, PS if pending sale or R if rental being held for income)	Type of Property	Present Market Value	Amount of Mortgages & Liens	Gross Rental Income	Mortgage Payments	Insurance, Maintenance, Taxes & Misc.	Net Rental Income
		$	$	$	$	$	$
	Totals	$	$	$	$	$	$

List any additional names under which credit has previously been received and indicate appropriate creditor name(s) and account number(s):

Alternate Name	Creditor Name	Account Number

Part 7
Line Break Down
A, Purchase Price (The price the borrower has agreed to pay to purchase the subject property

B, Alterations, improvements, repairs (The cost of any repairs or improvements to the property that are required by either the appraiser or sales contract)

C, Land (The cost of the land if purchased separately at a different time)

D, Refinance (Total of all liens to be paid off in refinance)

E, Estimate Pre-Paid Items

F, Estimate Closing Costs (Total Cost the borrower will pay to obtain the loan as disclosed
on the Good Faith Estimate)

G, PMI, MIP, and Funding Fee (Amount of Mortgage Insurance, Monthly Interest Payment or funding required *the borrower pays in cash

- PRIVATE Mortgage Insurance (PMI) (Insurance provided by nongovernmental insure t

protects lenders against loss if the borrower defaults) H, Discount (Amount of discount fee the borrower is paying) I, Total Costs (Add lines a-h)
J, Subordinate Financing (Amount of any other financing involved in this transaction) Usually The CLTV is limited to 90% combined loan-to-value (CLTV)
The relationship between the unpaid principal balances of all the mortgages on a property (£ and second usually) and the property's appraised value (or sales price, if it is lower).
K, Borrower's Closing Costs Paid by Seller (amount of dosing cost the seller has agreed to pay per the sales contract)
L, Other Credits explanation required one Example Cash Deposit paid toward property.. (Earnest Monies)
M, Loan Amount - Amount of the Loan (Exclude PMI, MIP, Funding Fee financed)
N, PMI, MPI. Funding Fee financed (   )
O, Loan Amount (add M&N)
P. Cash from/ to Borrower (Subtract J, K, L & O from *I)*
*subtract loan amount (o) from total cost (I) and subtract subordinate financing (J) Subtract borrowers closing cost paid by seller (K) subtract other credits, deposits on earnest money, plus other equity (I) The results is the amount of funds due or refunded at closing

Review and check

Part 8 DECLARATIONS (Cont).

√ Check for all this information on Loan Application
Declaration * Questions for Borrower and Co-Borrower line Break Down

GENERALLY, A "yes" to any of these questions (with the exception of having endorsed a note or paying alimony or child support) indicates a serious financial problem and may be reason to deny credit. A full explanation on a separate sheet must be attached to the application
A, Out Standing Judgments, against you
B, Bankruptcy within past 7 years
C, Foreclosures in the past 7 years
D, Are you a party to a law suit
E, Have you been directly or indirectly involved in a loan that resulted in foreclosure, transfer of title in lieu or judgment
F, Are you presently default or delinquent in any federal debt or any other financial

G, Are you obligated to pay alimony, child support or maintenance
H, Is any part of your down payment borrowed
I, Are you a co-maker or endorser on a note
J, Are you a US dozen
K, Are you a permanent resident alien
L, Do you intend to occupy this property as your primary resident
M, Have you had an ownership interest in a property in the past 3 years

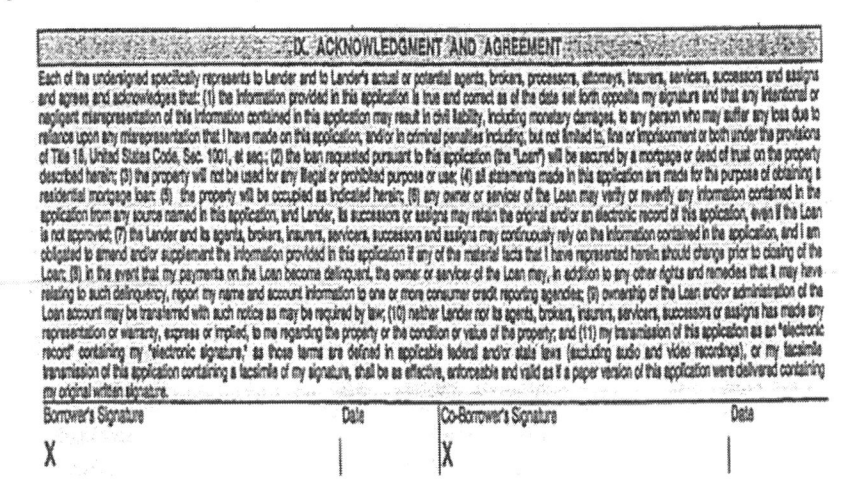

Part 9 Acknowledgement and Agreement Read the small print here

*The applicant is acknowledging and signing that all his/her statements are true and that the property will be or will not be the primary residence.

"Borrower's signature (Applicant (s) sign die application

- Interviewer's information (Name, Signature, Date, Phone Number, Name and Address of interviewers employer)

- It's important that the applicants understand that making false statements on this application's a federal crime.

X. INFORMATION FOR GOVERNMENT MONITORING PURPOSES

The following information is requested by the Federal Government for certain types of loans related to a dwelling in order to monitor the lender's compliance with equal credit opportunity, fair housing and home mortgage disclosure laws. You are not required to furnish this information, but are encouraged to do so. The law provides that a Lender may discriminate neither on the basis of this information, nor on whether you choose to furnish it. If you furnish the information, please provide both ethnicity and race. For race, you may check more than one designation. If you do not furnish ethnicity, race, or sex, under Federal regulations, this lender is required to note the information on the basis of visual observation or surname. If you do not wish to furnish the information, please check the box below. (Lender must review the above material to assure that the disclosures satisfy all requirements to which the lender is subject under applicable state law for the particular type of loan applied for.)

BORROWER	☐ I do not wish to furnish this information		CO-BORROWER	☐ I do not wish to furnish this information	
Ethnicity:	☐ Hispanic or Latino	☐ Not Hispanic or Latino	Ethnicity:	☐ Hispanic or Latino	☐ Not Hispanic or Latino
Race:	☐ American Indian or Alaska Native	☐ Asian ☒ Black or African American	Race:	☐ American Indian or Alaska Native	☐ Asian ☐ Black or African American
	☐ Native Hawaiian or Other Pacific Islander	☐ White		☐ Native Hawaiian or Other Pacific Islander	☐ White
Sex:	☐ Female	☒ Male	Sex:	☐ Female	☐ Male

To be Completed by Interviewer
This application was taken by:
☒ Face-to-face interview
☐ Mail
☐ Telephone
☐ Internet

Interviewer's Name (print or type): BETTY
Interviewer's Signature / Date
Interviewer's Phone Number (incl. area code): 000-000-0000

Name and Address of Interviewer's Employer
YOUR LENDING CO
111 JOHN ST
BLOOMINGTON, NY 111111
(P) 111-111-11111
(F) 222-222-22222

Freddie Mac Form 65 01/04
Calyx Form 1003 Loanapp3.frm 01/04
Page 3 of 4
Fannie Mae Form 1003 01/04

Part 10 Check

Information for Government Monitoring Purposes Borrower and Co-Borrower
- Ethnicity Hispanic non-Hispanic
- Race (, Black, Caucasian, Native American etc._
- Sex (male Female)
- Interviewer's information (Name, Signature, Date, Phone Number, Name and Address of interviewer's employer

Part 10 Information for the Government Monitoring Purposes

The following information is requested by the Federal Government for certain types of loans related to a dwelling in order to monitor the Lender's compliance with equal credit opportunity, fair housing and home mortgage disclosure laws. You are not required to furnish this information, but are encouraged to do so. The law provides that a lender may not discriminate either on the basis of this information, or on whether you choose to furnish it. If you furnish the information, please provide both ethnicity and race. For race, you may check more than one designation.

*Please check all boxes and fill in the correct information
Information is for borrower(s) and Co-Borrower(s) if any.

*Please check the box if the Borrower(s) and Co-Borrower(s) do not wish to furnish this information.

Interviewers Name (print or type)
Name and address of Interviewers employer
Interviewer's Signature and Phone number
Date the Document

MORTGAGE FORMS AND DISCLOSURE NOTICES

Important Notice to Homebuyers

U.S. Department of Housing and Urban Development
Office of Housing - Federal Housing Commissioner

You **must** read this entire document at the time you apply for the loan.
Return one copy to lender as proof of notification and keep one copy for your records.

Condition of Property

The property you are buying is not HUD/FHA approved and HUD/FHA does not warrant the condition or the value of the property. An appraisal will be performed to estimate the value of the property, but this appraisal does not guarantee that the house is free of defects. You should inspect the property yourself very carefully or hire a professional inspection service to inspect the property for you. If you have a professional home inspection service perform an inspection of the property, you may include some of the cost of the inspection in your mortgage.

Interest Rate and Discount Points

HUD does not regulate the interest rate or the discount points that may be paid by you or the seller or other third party. You should shop around to be sure you are satisfied with the loan terms offered and with the service reputation of the lender you have chosen.

The interest rate, any discount points and the length of time the lender will honor the loan terms are all negotiated between you and the lender.

The seller can pay the discount points, or a portion thereof, if you and the seller agree to such an arrangement.

Lenders may agree to guarantee or "lock-in" the loan terms for a definite period of time (i.e., 15, 30, 60 days, etc.) or may permit your loan to be determined by future market conditions, also known as "floating". Lenders may require a fee to lock in the interest rate or the terms of the loan, but must provide a written agreement covering a minimum of 15 days before the anticipated closing. Your agreement with the lender will determine the degree, if any, that the interest rate and discount points may rise before closing.

If the lender determines you are eligible for the mortgage, your agreement with the seller may require you to complete the transaction or lose your deposit on the property.

Don't Commit Loan Fraud

It is important for you to understand that you are required to provide complete and accurate information when applying for a mortgage loan.

Do not falsify information about your income or assets.

Disclose all loans and debts (including money that may have been borrowed to make the downpayment).

Do not provide false letters-of-credit, cash-on-hand statements, gift letters or sweat equity letters.

Do not accept funds to be used for your downpayment from any other party (seller, real estate salesperson, builder, etc.).

Do not falsely certify that a property will be used for your primary residence when you are actually going to use it as a rental property.

Do not act as a "strawbuyer" (somebody who purchases a property for another person and then transfers title of the property to that person), nor should you give that person personal or credit information for them to use in any such scheme.

Do not apply for a loan by assuming the identity of another person.

Do not sign documents in "blank."

Penalties for Loan Fraud: Federal laws provide severe penalties for fraud, misreprestation, or conspiracy to influence wrongly the issuance of mortgage insurance by HUD. You can be subject to a possible prison term and fine of up to $10,000 for providing false information. Additionally, you could be prohibited from obtaining a HUD-insured loan for an indefinite period.

Report Loan Fraud: If you are aware of any fraud in HUD programs or if an individual tries to persuade you to make false statements on a loan application, you should report the matter by calling your nearest HUD office or the HUD Regional Inspector General, or call the HUD Hotline on 1 (800) 347-3735.

Warning: It is a crime to knowingly make false statements to the United States Government on this or any similar form. Penalties upon conviction can include a fine and imprisonment. For details see: Title 18 U.S Code Section 1001 and Section 1010.

Discrimination

If you believe you have been subject to discrimination because of race, color, religion, sex, handicap, familial status, or national origin, you should call HUD's Fair Housing & Equal Opportunity Complaint Hotline: 1 (800) 669-9777.

About Prepayment

This notice is to advise you of the requirements that must be followed to accomplish a prepayment of your mortgage, and to prevent accrual of any interest after the date of prepayment.

You may prepay any or all of the outstanding indebtedness due under your mortgage at any time, without penalty. However, to avoid the accrual of interest on any prepayment, the prepayment must be received on the installment due date (the first day of the month) if the lender stated this policy in its response to a request for a payoff figure.

Otherwise, you may be required to pay interest on the amount prepaid through the end of the month. The lender can refuse to accept prepayment on any date other than the installment due date.

Previous editions are obsolete

Note: If you are a first-time homebuyer and you received approved homeownership counseling, you may be entitled to a reduced upfront mortgage insurance premium. Ask your lender for details.

Who May be Eligible for a Refund?

Premium Refund: You may be eligible for a refund of a portion of the insurance premium if you paid an upfront mortgage insurance premium at settlement.

Review your settlement papers or check with your mortgage company to determine if you paid an upfront premium.

Exceptions:

Assumptions: When a FHA insured loan is assumed the insurance remains in force (the seller receives no refund). The owper(s) of the property at the time the insurance is terminated is entitled to any refund.

FHA to FHA Refinance: When a FHA insured loan is refinanced, the refund from the old premium may be applied toward the upfront premium required for the new loan.

Claims: When a mortgage company submits a claim to HUD for insurance benefits, no refund is due the homeowner.

How are Refunds Determined?

The FHA Commissioner determines how much of the upfront premium is refunded when loans are terminated. Refunds are based on the number of months the loan is insured. After 84 months (7 years) no refund is due the homeowner.

How are Refunds Processed?

1. Mortgage company notifies HUD of insurance termination.
2. If you are eligible for a refund, HUD will either request Treasury to issue you a check directly or will send you an Application for Premium Refund (form HUD-27050-B).
3. Read the application carefully, sign, have it notarized, and attach proof of ownership at insurance termination.
4. Return application to the address shown on the HUD-27050-B.
5. HUD will request Treasury to issue a check if no additional information is needed.

How to Follow-Up

If you do not receive an application within 45 days after you have paid off your loan, check with your mortgage company to confirm that they have sent HUD a request for termination. If they confirm that the correct termination information was sent, contact HUD.

If you do not receive a refund or any other documentation from HUD within 60 days from the date you mailed your application, contact HUD immediately.

How to Contact HUD

By Phone:
800 697-6967
8:30 AM to 8:30 PM (EST)
Monday through Friday

By Mail:
U.S. Department of Housing & Urban Development
PO Box 23699
Washington, DC 20026-3699

Note: All inquiries should include your name, 10-digit FHA case number, paid in full date, property address, and a daytime phone number. Record your FHA case number here for future reference.

Important: The rules governing the eligibility for premium refunds are based on the financial status of the FHA insurance fund and are **subject to change.**

SI USTED HABLA ESPANOL Y TIENE DIFICULTAD LEYENDO O HABLANDO INGLES, POR FAVOR LLAME A ESTE NUMERO TELEFONICO 800 697-6967.

You, the borrower(s), must be certain that you understand the transaction. Seek professional advice if you are uncertain.

Acknowledgment: I acknowledge that I have read and received a copy of this notice at the time of loan application. This notice does not constitute a contract or binding agreement. It is designed to provide current HUD/FHA policy regarding refunds.

Signature & Date:

X_____

Signature & Date:

X_____

Signature & Date:

X_____

Signature & Date:

X_____

Previous editions are obsolete

Uniform Loan Submission Sheet

Lender
Lender: _____ Contact: _____
Addr: _____   Phone #: _____
C/S/Z: _____   Fax #: _____

Submitting Broker/Lender
YOUR LENDING CO
111 JOHN ST
BLOOMINGTON, NY 111111
Agent: BETTY   Phone#: 000-000-0000
Processor: _____   Fax#: _____

Appraisal Company
Appraiser: _____ Phone#: _____
License#: _____   Fax#: _____

Escrow Company
Officer: _____   Phone#: _____
Escrow#: _____   Fax#: _____
Estimated Close of Escrow: 02/10/2000

Title Company
Officer: _____   Phone#: _____
Title#: _____   Fax#: _____

Loan Summary and Terms

Applicant(s):
SAMPLE ONLY BORROWER, MR

Property Address:
123 JOHN ST
JOHNSTOWN, NY 12345
County: Schenectady   Census Tract: _____

Borr SS#: 123-45-6789   CoBorr SS#: _____
Program: _____   Pgm Code: _____
[✓] 1st TD   [✓] Purchase   [ ] Ref/NoCash   [ ] 2nd Home
[ ] 2nd TD   [ ] Ref/CashOut   [✓] OwnerOcc   [ ] Investment

Prop Type: _____   Units: 1   Full Doc: [ ]   Other: [ ]
Impounds: [ ] Taxes [ ] Hazard [ ] MMI/PMI [ ] Flood

Type of Buydown: _____
Adjustment Period: _____
Index: ____%   AdjCap: ____%
Margin: ____%   PmtCap: ____%
Other: _____   LifeCap: ____%

Loan Amount: $ 135,000
Note Rate: 6.500 %
Quality Rate: 6.500 %
Term (in months): 360
Amortization: _____

[✓] Float
[ ] LockedOn: _____   MI: [ ] Yes [✓] No
# of Days: _____   Type: _____
Expires: _____

Sales Price: $ 150,000
Appraisal: $ _____
Down Payment: $ 15,000
LTV: 90.000 %
LTV(Combined): 90.000 %

Demand

	Lender	Broker		Borrower	
Loan Origination	__%+ __	1.000%+ __	1,350.00	1.000%+ __	1,350.00
Loan Discount	__%+ __	__%+ __		__%+ __	
Yield Spread Premium	__%+ __	__%+ __		__%+ __	
Appraisal Fee		Paid/Due	300.00		300.00
Credit Report Fee		Paid/Due	25.00		25.00
Processing Fee		Paid/Due	500.00		500.00
Loan Document		Paid/Due			
		Paid/Due			
		Paid/Due			
		Paid/Due			
		Paid/Due			
		Paid/Due			
Total		Paid/Due	2,175.00		2,175.00

Comments/Other Instructions

Name: Mr. Borrower   Signature: *MR Borrower*   Date: 07/07/2008

TRUTH-IN-LENDING DISCLOSURE STATEMENT
(THIS IS NEITHER A CONTRACT NOR A COMMITMENT TO LEND)

Applicants:	SAMPLE ONLY BORROWER, MR	Prepared By:	YOUR LENDING CO 111 JOHN ST
Property Address:	123 JOHN ST JOHNSTOWN, NY 12345		BLOOMINGTON, NY 111111 111-111-11111
Application No:	MR.BORROWER	Date Prepared:	01/01/2000

ANNUAL PERCENTAGE RATE	FINANCE CHARGE	AMOUNT FINANCED	TOTAL OF PAYMENTS
The cost of your credit as a yearly rate	The dollar amount the credit will cost you	The amount of credit provided to you or on your behalf	The amount you will have paid after making all payments as scheduled
6.500 %	$ 172,186.36	$ 135,000.00	$ 307,186.36

☐ **REQUIRED DEPOSIT:** The annual percentage rate does not take into account your required deposit

PAYMENTS: Your payment schedule will be:

Number of Payments	Amount of Payments **	When Payments Are Due	Number of Payments	Amount of Payments **	When Payments Are Due	Number of Payments	Amount of Payments **	When Payments Are Due
		Monthly Beginning:			Monthly Beginning:			Monthly Beginning:
359	853.29	03/01/2000						
1	855.25	02/01/2030						

☐ **DEMAND FEATURE:** This obligation has a demand feature.
☐ **VARIABLE RATE FEATURE:** This loan contains a variable rate feature. A variable rate disclosure has been provided earlier.

CREDIT LIFE/CREDIT DISABILITY: Credit life insurance and credit disability insurance are not required to obtain credit, and will not be provided unless you sign and agree to pay the additional cost.

Type	Premium	Signature
Credit Life		I want credit life insurance. Signature:
Credit Disability		I want credit disability insurance. Signature:
Credit Life and Disability		I want credit life and disability insurance. Signature:

INSURANCE: The following insurance is required to obtain credit:
☐ Credit life insurance ☐ Credit disability ☐ Property insurance ☐ Flood insurance
You may obtain the insurance from anyone you want that is acceptable to creditor
☐ If you purchase ☐ property ☐ flood insurance from creditor you will pay $ _____ for a one year term.
SECURITY: You are giving a security interest in:
☐ The goods or property being purchased ☐ Real property you already own.
FILING FEES: $
LATE CHARGE: If a payment is more than _____ days late, you will be charged _____ % of the payment
PREPAYMENT: If you pay off early, you
☐ may ☐ will not have to pay a penalty.
☐ may ☐ will not be entitled to a refund of part of the finance charge.
ASSUMPTION: Someone buying your property
☐ may ☐ may, subject to conditions ☐ may not assume the remainder of your loan on the original terms.
See your contract documents for any additional information about nonpayment, default, any required repayment in full before the scheduled date and prepayment refunds and penalties.
☐ * means an estimate ☐ all dates and numerical disclosures except the late payment disclosures are estimates.
* * NOTE: The Payments shown above include reserve deposits for Mortgage Insurance (if applicable), but exclude Property Taxes and Insurance.

THE UNDERSIGNED ACKNOWLEDGES RECEIVING A COMPLETED COPY OF THIS DISCLOSURE.

_____ _____
SAMPLE ONLY BORROWER, MR (Applicant) (Date)   (Applicant) (Date)

_____ _____
(Applicant) (Date)   (Applicant) (Date)

_____
(Lender) (Date)

Uniform Underwriting and Transmittal Summary

I. Borrower and Property Information

Borrower Name: _____ SSN: _____
Co-Borrower Name: _____ SSN: _____
Property Address: _____

Property Type
- ☐ 1 unit
- ☐ 2–4 units
- ☐ Condominium
- ☐ PUD ☐ Co-op
- ☐ Manufactured Housing
  - ☐ Single Wide ☐ Multiwide

Project Classification
- ☐ A/II Condo ☐ E PUD ☐ 1 Co-op
- ☐ B/II Condo ☐ F PUD ☐ 2 Co-op
- ☐ C/I Condo

Project Name: _____

Occupancy Status
- ☐ Primary Residence
- ☐ Second Home
- ☐ Investment Property

Additional Property Information
Number of Units: _____
Sales Price: $ _____
Appraised Value: $ _____

Property Rights
- ☐ Fee Simple
- ☐ Leasehold

II. Mortgage Information

Loan Type
- ☐ Conventional
- ☐ FHA
- ☐ VA
- ☐ USDA/RHS

Amortization Type
- ☐ Fixed-Rate—Monthly Payments
- ☐ Fixed-Rate—Biweekly Payments
- ☐ Balloon
- ☐ ARM (type) _____
- ☐ Other (specify) _____

Loan Purpose
- ☐ Purchase
- ☐ Cash-Out Refinance
- ☐ Limited Cash-Out Refinance (Fannie)
- ☐ No Cash-Out Refinance (Freddie)
- ☐ Home Improvement
- ☐ Construction to Permanent

Lien Position
- ☐ First Mortgage
  Amount of Subordinate Financing
  $ _____
  (If HELOC, include balance and credit limit)
- ☐ Second Mortgage

Note Information
Original Loan Amount: $ _____
Initial P&I Payment: $ _____
Initial Note Rate: _____ %
Loan Term (in months): _____

Mortgage Originator
- ☐ Seller
- ☐ Broker
- ☐ Correspondent
Broker/Correspondent Name and Company Name: _____

Buydown
- ☐ Yes
- ☐ No
Terms: _____

If Second Mortgage
Owner of First Mortgage
- ☐ Fannie Mae ☐ Freddie Mac
- ☐ Seller/Other
Original Loan Amount of First Mortgage
$ _____

III. Underwriting Information

Underwriter's Name: _____ Appraiser's Name/License #: _____ Appraisal Company Name: _____

Stable Monthly Income

	Borrower	Co-Borrower	Total
Base Income	$	$	$
Other Income	$	$	$
Positive Cash Flow (subject property)	$	$	$
Total Income	$	$	$

Qualifying Ratios
Primary Housing Expense/Income: _____ %
Total Obligations/Income: _____ %
Debt-to-Housing Gap Ratio (Freddie): _____ %

Qualifying Rate
- ☐ Note Rate
- ☐ _____ % Above Note Rate
- ☐ _____ % Below Note Rate
- ☐ Bought-Down Rate _____ %
- ☐ Other _____ %

Risk Assessment
- ☐ Manual Underwriting
- ☐ AUS
  - ☐ DU ☐ LP ☐ Other
  AUS Recommendation: _____
  DU Case ID/LP AUS Key#: _____
  LP Doc Class (Freddie): _____
Representative Credit/Indicator Score: _____

Loan-to-Value Ratios
LTV: _____ %
CLTV/TLTV: _____ %
HCLTV/HTLTV: _____ %

Level of Property Review
- ☐ Exterior/Interior
- ☐ Exterior Only
- ☐ No Appraisal
Form Number: _____

Escrow (T&I)
- ☐ Yes ☐ No

Community Lending/Affordable Housing Initiative ☐ Yes ☐ No
Home Buyers/Homeownership Education Certificate in file ☐ Yes ☐ No

Present Housing Payment: $ _____
Proposed Monthly Payments
Borrower's Primary Residence
First Mortgage P&I: $ _____
Second Mortgage P&I: $ _____
Hazard Insurance: $ _____
Taxes: $ _____
Mortgage Insurance
HOA Fees: $ _____
Lease/Ground Rent: $ _____
Other: $ _____
Total Primary Housing Expense: $ _____
Other Obligations
Negative Cash Flow (subject property): $ _____
All Other Monthly Payments: $ _____
Total All Monthly Payments: $ _____

Borrower Funds to Close
Required: $ _____
Verified Assets: $ _____

Source of Funds: _____
No. of Months Reserves: _____
Interested Party Contributions: _____ %

Underwriter Comments
_____
_____
_____
_____
_____
_____
_____

IV. Seller, Contract, and Contact Information

Seller Name: _____
Seller Address: _____
Seller No.: _____ Investor Loan No.: _____
Seller Loan No.: _____
Master Commitment No.: _____
Contract No.: _____

Contact Name: _____
Contact Title: _____
Contact Phone Number: _____ ext. _____
Contact Signature: _____
Date: _____

GOOD FAITH ESTIMATE

Applicants:	SAMPLE ONLY BORROWER, MR	Application No:	MR.BORROWER
Property Addr:	123 JOHN ST, JOHNSTOWN, NY 12345	Date Prepared:	01/01/2000
Prepared By:	YOUR LENDING CO Ph. 111-111-11111	Loan Program:	ADJUSTABLE
	111 JOHN ST, BLOOMINGTON, NY 111111		

The information provided below reflects estimates of the charges which you are likely to incur at the settlement of your loan. The fees listed are estimates-actual charges may be more or less. Your transaction may not involve a fee for every item listed. The numbers listed beside the estimates generally correspond to the numbered lines contained in the HUD-1 settlement statement which you will be receiving at settlement. The HUD-1 settlement statement will show you the actual cost for items paid at settlement.

Total Loan Amount $ 135,000   Interest Rate: 6.500 %   Term: 360 / 360 mths

800	ITEMS PAYABLE IN CONNECTION WITH LOAN:		
801	Loan Origination Fee 1.000%	$	1,350.00
802	Loan Discount		
803	Appraisal Fee		300.00
804	Credit Report		25.00
805	Lender's Inspection Fee		
808	Mortgage Broker Fee		
809	Tax Related Service Fee		78.00
810	Processing Fee		500.00
811	Underwriting Fee		699.00
812	Wire Transfer Fee		

1100	TITLE CHARGES:		
1101	Closing or Escrow Fee	$	165.00
1105	Document Preparation Fee		
1106	Notary Fees		
1107	Attorney Fees		250.00
1108	Title Insurance		290.00

1200	GOVERNMENT RECORDING & TRANSFER CHARGES:		
1201	Recording Fees	$	65.00
1202	City/County Tax/Stamps		
1203	State Tax/Stamps		

1300	ADDITIONAL SETTLEMENT CHARGES:		
1302	Pest Inspection	$	

	Estimated Closing Costs		3,722.00
900	ITEMS REQUIRED BY LENDER TO BE PAID IN ADVANCE:		
901	Interest for 15 days @ $ 24.3750 per day	$	365.63
902	Mortgage Insurance Premium		
903	Hazard Insurance Premium		80.00
904			
905	VA Funding Fee		

1000	RESERVES DEPOSITED WITH LENDER:			
1001	Hazard Insurance Premiums	months @ $	40.00 per month	$
1002	Mortgage Ins. Premium Reserves	months @ $	per month	
1003	School Tax	months @ $	per month	
1004	Taxes and Assessment Reserves	2 months @ $	197.00 per month	394.00
1005	Flood Insurance Reserves	months @ $	per month	
		months @ $	per month	
		months @ $	per month	

	Estimated Prepaid Items/Reserves	839.63
TOTAL ESTIMATED SETTLEMENT CHARGES		4,561.63

TOTAL ESTIMATED FUNDS NEEDED TO CLOSE:		TOTAL ESTIMATED MONTHLY PAYMENT:	
Purchase Price/Payoff (+)	150,000.00	Principal & Interest	853.29
Loan Amount (-)	135,000.00	Other Financing (P & I)	
New First Mortgage(-)		Hazard Insurance	40.00
Est. Closing Costs (+)	3,722.00	Real Estate Taxes	197.00
New 2nd Mtg Closing Costs(+)		Mortgage Insurance	
Est. Prepaid Items/Reserves (+)	839.63	Homeowner Assn. Dues	
Amount Paid by Seller (-)		Other	
Cash Deposit	(1,000.00)		
Total Est. Funds needed to close	18,561.63	Total Monthly Payment	1,090.29

These estimates are provided pursuant to the Real Estate Settlement Procedures Act of 1974, as amended (RESPA). Additional information can be found in the HUD Special Information Booklet, which is to be provided to you by your mortgage broker or lender. If your application is to purchase residential real property and the lender will take a first lien on the property. The undersigned acknowledges receipt of the booklet "Settlement Costs," and if applicable the Consumer Handbook on ARM Mortgages.

Mr Borrower 2008

Applicant SAMPLE ONLY BORROWER, MR   Date   Applicant   Date

DISCLOSURE NOTICES

Applicant(s)	Property Address

☐ OCCUPANCY STATEMENT

This is to certify that I/We ☐ do ☐ do not intend to occupy the subject property as my/our principal residence. I/We hereby certify under penalty of U.S. Criminal Code Section 1010 Title 18 U.S.C., that the above statement submitted for the purpose of obtaining mortgage insurance under the National Housing Act is true and correct.

FAIR CREDIT REPORTING ACT

An investigation will be made as to the credit standing of all individuals seeking credit in this application. The nature and scope of any investigation will be furnished to you upon written request made within a reasonable period of time. In the event of denied credit due to an unfavorable consumer report, you will be advised of the identity of the Consumer Reporting Agency making such report and of right to request within sixty (60) days the reason for the adverse action, pursuant to provisions of section 615(b) of the Fair Credit Reporting Act.

EQUAL CREDIT OPPORTUNITY ACT

The Equal Credit Opportunity Act prohibits creditors from discriminating against credit applicants on the basis of race, color, religion, national origin, sex, marital status, age (provided that the applicant has the capacity to enter into a binding contract); because all or part of the applicant's income derives from any public assistance program; or because the applicant has in good faith exercised any right under the Consumer Credit Protection Act. Income which you receive as alimony, child support or separate maintenance need not be disclosed to this creditor unless you choose to rely on such sources to qualify for the loan. Income from these and other sources, including part-time or temporary employment, will not be discounted by this lender because of your sex or marital status. However, we will consider very carefully the stability and probable continuity of any income you disclose to us. The Federal Agency that administers compliance with this law concerning this creditor is:

☐ RIGHT TO FINANCIAL PRIVACY ACT

I/we acknowledge that this is notice to me/us as required by The Right to Financial Privacy Act of 1978 that the Veterans Administration (in the case of a VA Loan) or Department of Housing and Urban Development (in the case of an FHA Loan) has a right of access to financial records held by financial institutions in connection with the consideration or administration of assistance to me/us. Financial records involving my/our transactions will be available to the VA (in the case of a VA Loan) or to HUD (in the case of an FHA Loan) without further notice or authorization but will not be disclosed or released to another government agency or department without my/our consent, except as required or permitted by law.

☐ INFORMATION DISCLOSURE AUTHORIZATION

I/We hereby authorize you to release to _____ for verification purposes, information concerning: ☐ Employment History, dates, title(s), income, hours worked, etc. ☐ Banking (checking & savings) account of record. ☐ Mortgage loan rating, (opening date, high credit, payment amount, loan balance and payment. ☐ Any information deemed necessary in connection with consumer credit report for real estate transaction. This information is for the confidential use of this lender in compiling a mortgage loan credit report. A copy of this authorization may be deemed to be the equivalent of the original and may be used as a duplicate original.

☐ ANTI-COERCION STATEMENT

The insurance laws of this state provide that the lender may not require the applicant to take insurance through any particular insurance agent or company to protect the mortgaged property. The applicant, subject to the rules adopted by the Insurance Commissioner, has the right to have the insurance placed with an insurance agent or company of his choice, provided the company meets the requirements of the lender. The lender has the right to designate reasonable financial requirements as to the company and the adequacy of the coverage.

I have read the foregoing statement, or the rules of the Insurance Commissioner relative thereto, and understand my rights and privileges and those of the lender relative to the placing of such insurance.

I have selected the following agencies to write the insurance covering the property described above:

Insurance Co. Name:
    Agent:

☐ FLOOD INSURANCE NOTIFICATION

Federal regulations require us to inform you that the property used as security for this loan is located in an area identified by the U.S. Secretary of Housing & Urban Development as having special flood hazards and that in the event of damage to the property caused by flooding in a Federally-declared disaster, Federal disaster relief assistance, if authorized, will be available for the property.

At the closing you will be asked to acknowledge your receipt of this information. If you have any questions concerning this notice, kindly contact your loan officer.

IMPORTANT: Please notify your insurance agent that the "loss payee" clause for the mortgagee on both the hazard and flood insurance must read as follows, unless otherwise advised:

☐ CONSUMER HANDBOOK ON ADJUSTABLE RATE MORTGAGES

I/We hereby acknowledge receipt from _____ of a copy of the book titled "CONSUMER HANDBOOK ON ADJUSTABLE RATE MORTGAGES" published by the Federal Reserve Board and the Federal Home Loan Bank Board which is provided in addition to other required adjustable rate mortgage disclosures.

I/We hereby certify that I/we have read the Notices set forth above and fully understand all of the above.

Mr. Borrower	2008		
APPLICANT	DATE	APPLICANT	DATE

APPLICANT	DATE	APPLICANT	

MORTGAGE LOAN COMMITMENT

Applicants:	SAMPLE ONLY BORROWER, MR	Lender:	
Property Address:	123 JOHN ST JOHNSTOWN, NY 12345		
Application No:	MR.BORROWER	Date Prepared:	

It is a pleasure to notify you that your application for a first mortgage loan has been approved subject to the following matters set forth below. See Good Faith Estimate of Settlement Charges for any related closing costs.

AMOUNT, TERMS AND FEES

Amount of Loan: $	135,000	Contract Interest Rate:	6.500 %	LTV:	90.000 %
Terms/Due In:	360/360	Commitment Expires:		CLTV:	90.000 %

REPAYMENT TERMS

EVIDENCE OF TITLE

The following Evidence of Title is to be provided to the Lender and must indicate no liens, encumbrances, or any adverse covenants or conditions to title unless approved by Lender. The Evidence of Title must be issued from a firm or source, and in a form, acceptable to Lender.

Borrower will be charged for the cost of providing such title and the cost of recording documents, all of which will be ordered by Lender unless requested otherwise.

ADDITIONAL REQUIRED ITEMS OR CONDITIONS

SEE NEXT PAGE INSTRUCTIONS

The Continuation of Commitment Conditions is made a part of this Commitment. Please sign and return Lender's COPY of this Commitment along with any required fee and items requested, to the lender at the: ☐ above address ☐ following address, within _____ days of date hereof, or at the option of Lender, this commitment shall become null and void.
I (WE) hereby accept the terms and Conditions of this Commitment.

COMMITMENT ISSUED BY: ADDRESS:

Mr. Borrower 2008

Authorized Signature Date

Applicant SAMPLE ONLY BORROWER, MR Date   Applicant Date

Applicant Date   Applicant Date

CONDITIONAL LOAN APPROVAL

1. The undersigned ☐ Mortgage Banker ☐ Mortgage Broker ("Lender") has made a preliminary review of the ability of:
2. _____ ("Buyer") to qualify for a real estate loan.
3. Based on the information provided, Buyer is conditionally approved for a real estate loan on the following terms:

4. Amount requested: $ _____
5. Loan Program: ☐ FHA ☐ VA ☐ Conventional ☐ Other, explain: _____
6. Interest Rate: _____ Buyer ☐ has ☐ has NOT locked in interest rate.
7. If interest rate is locked, expiration date: _____
8. Origination Fee/Points: _____ Discount Points: _____

9. Note: AAR Contracts require a Conditional Loan Approval ("CLA") based on a loan application and Trimerged
10. Residential Credit Report ("TMRCR").
11. Is this Conditional Loan Approval based on the following?
12. Yes No
13. ☐ ☐ A completed loan application. If yes, date completed: _____
14. ☐ ☐ Review of a Trimerged Residential Credit Report (TMRCR).
15. ☐ ☐ If loan program is a FHA or VA loan and an AAR Residential Resale Purchase Contract has been executed, a
16. determination that the loan costs Seller agrees to pay pursuant to lines 80-82 of the Contract are sufficient to obtain
17. the loan? ☐ Not Applicable
18. ☐ ☐ Determination that Buyer's credit information meets guidelines of loan program referenced in line 5.
19. ☐ ☐ Determination that Buyer's income/ratios are within lending guidelines for this loan program.
20. ☐ ☐ Identification of the Buyer's ability to repay the loan. Explain _____
21. ☐ ☐ Identification and verification of the source of funds necessary to close, which is _____

22. Additional questions:
23. Yes No
24. ☐ ☐ Could Buyer's source of funds necessary to close cause a delay in closing?
25. If yes, explain: _____
26. ☐ ☐ Has Buyer received an automated loan approval?
27. ☐ ☐ Has Buyer received a Good Faith Estimate?
28. ☐ ☐ Has the appraisal fee been collected?
29. ☐ ☐ Has the appraisal been ordered? If yes, date ordered _____

30. Buyer ☐ is ☐ is not relying on the sale or lease of property to qualify for this loan.
31. List all conditions to loan approval: _____
32. _____
33. _____
34. _____
35. _____

36. This report is not a "commitment" or "final approval" of Buyer's ability to qualify for a real estate loan, which may be affected
37. by any material change in the Buyer's financial status from the information provided or by adverse property conditions.

38. Company Name: _____ License Number: _____
39. Address: _____
40. _____
41. Phone: _____ Fax: _____
42. Loan Officer: _____ Title: _____
43. Signature: _____ Date: _____

44. BUYER REPRESENTS THAT THE INFORMATION PROVIDED TO LENDER IS COMPLETE AND ACCURATE TO THE BEST OF BUYER'S
45. KNOWLEDGE. BUYER AUTHORIZES LENDER AND ANY BROKER TO MAKE THE ABOVE INFORMATION AVAILABLE IN CONNECTION
46. WITH THE BUYER'S PURCHASE OR ATTEMPT TO PURCHASE REAL PROPERTY AND ACKNOWLEDGES A RECEIPT HEREOF.

47. *Mr. Borrower* _____
    BUYER'S SIGNATURE   BUYER'S SIGNATURE
48. XX-XX-2008 _____
    DATE   DATE

INTEREST RATE LOCK-IN CONFIRMATION AGREEMENT

Borrower(s) Name: __Mr. Borrower__   Date of Lock-In: __XX-XX-2008__

Property Address: __123 John street__

__Need a home Lane, USA__

I/We have applied for a mortgage loan on the above mentioned property and request the following loan lock terms:

Loan Type: __Conv__   Loan Term: __30 years__

Loan Amount: __249,000__   Interest Rate: __7.25__ % __Fixed__

Index: _____   Margin: _____   Floor Rate: _____

Payment/Rate Adjustments: ____6 Months   ____Annual   ____Other

Annual or Other Adjustment Cap: _____   Life Cap: _____

Loan Origination Fee: _____   Discount Points _____

Yield Spread Premium: _____   Lock-in Fee: _____

Lock Term: __30 yr Fixed__   Expiration Date: _____

Comments/Limitations: _____

This lock-in agreement is not a commitment or agreement to grant your loan request or a loan approval. The loan must be fully underwritten and all conditions must be met prior to the loan closing. It is important that you provide all requested documentation in a timely manner. Lock-in terms will remain in effect through the expiration date except as noted below.

The locked-in interest rate and terms apply solely to the type of mortgage loan for which you have applied and have requested this lock-in for, and has been set as a result of the repayment term, loan amount, program, property and anticipated closing date. You acknowledge and understand that in the event that any of these items are changed, the locked-in interest rate and terms above may no longer be valid and a new lock-in agreement will have to be entered into and another lock-in fee may be charged.

Mr. Borrower	XX-XX-2008
Borrower	Date

Borrower	Date

Broker/Lender Representative Name (Printed)

Broker/Lender Representative Signature	Date

Form RD 1940-43
(Rev. 8-00)

UNITED STATES DEPARTMENT OF AGRICULTURE

| |Rural Housing Service
| |Rural Business-Cooperative Service
| |Rural Utilities Service

NOTICE OF RIGHT TO CANCEL

Type Loan
Amount Financed
$

To:

Your Right to Cancel You are entering into a transaction that will result in a mortgage on your home. You have a legal right under Federal law to cancel this transaction, without cost, until midnight of the third business day after, whichever of the following events occurs last:

(1) the date of closing of the transaction,

(2) the date you received your Truth in Lending disclosure,

(3) the date you received this notice of your right to cancel.

If you cancel the transaction, the mortgage is also canceled. Within 20 calendar days after we receive your notice, we must take the steps necessary to reflect the fact that the mortgage on your home has been canceled, and we must return to you any money or property you have given to us or to anyone else in connection with this transaction.

You may keep any money or property we have given you until we have done the things mentioned above, but you must then offer to return the money or property. If it is impractical or unfair for you to return the property, you must offer its reasonable value. You may offer to return the property at your home or at the location of the property. Money must be returned to the address below. If we do not take possession of the money or property within 20 calendar days of your offer, you may keep it without further obligation.

How to Cancel

If you decide to cancel this transaction, you may do so by notifying the Agency as indicated above in writing, at

USDA,

(Field Office Address)

You may use any written statement that is signed and dated by you and states your intention to cancel, or you may use this notice by dating and signing below. Keep one copy of this notice because it contains important information about your rights.

If you cancel by mail or telegram, you must send the notice no later than midnight of _____ ,20____ (or midnight of the third business day following the latest of the events listed above). If you send or deliver your written notice to cancel some other way, it must be delivered to the above address no later than that time.

I WISH TO CANCEL

_____   _____
              (Signature)   *(Date)*

According to the Paperwork Reduction Act of 1995, no persons are required to respond to a collection of information unless it displays a valid OMB control number. The valid OMB control number for this information collection is 0575-0172. The time required to complete this information collection is estimated to average 5 minutes per response, including the time for reviewing instructions, searching existing data sources, gathering and maintaining the data needed, and completing and reviewing the collection of information.

CREDIT REPORT AUTHORIZATION AND RELEASE

Authorization is hereby granted to **American Capital Mortgage Co., Inc.** to obtain a standard factual data credit report through a credit reporting agency chosen by **American Capital Mortgage Co., Inc.**

My signature below authorizes the release to the credit reporting agency a copy of my credit application, and authorizes **American Capital Mortgage Co., Inc.** or any credit reporting agency to obtain information regarding my employment, savings accounts, and outstanding credit accounts (mortgages, auto loans, personal loans, charge cards, credit unions, etc.). Authorization is further granted to **American Capital Mortgage Co., Inc.** or any credit reporting agency to use a Photostat reproduction of this authorization if necessary to obtain any information regarding the above mentioned information.

Applicants hereby request a copy of credit report obtained with any possible derogatory information to be sent to the address of present residence, and holds **American Capital Mortgage Co., Inc.** and any credit reporting organization harmless in so mailing the copy requested.

Any reproduction of this credit report authorization and release made by reliable means (for example, photocopy or facsimile) is considered an original.

Borrower _____   Date _____

Co-borrower _____   Date _____

NAME: _____   SOCIAL SECURITY NO. _____

ADDRESS: _____

_____

_____

NAME: _____   SOCIAL SECURITY NO. _____

ADDRESS: _____

_____

_____

NOTICE TO THE HOME LOAN APPLICANT
CREDIT SCORE INFORMATION DISCLOSURE

APPLICANT(S) NAME AND ADDRESS	LENDER NAME AND ADDRESS
	First Equity Financial 1072 Leroy Ln. Suite 100 Walnut Creek, CA 94597 (P)925-947-1448 (F)925-947-1363

In connection with your application for a home loan, the lender must disclose to you the score that a credit bureau distributed to users and the lender used in connection with your home loan, and the key factors affecting your credit scores.

The credit score is a computer-generated summary calculated at the time of the request and based on information a credit bureau or lender has on file. The scores are based on data about your credit history and payment patterns. Credit scores are important because they are used to assist the lender in determining whether you will obtain a loan. They may also be used to determine what interest rate you may be offered on the mortgage. Credit scores can change over time, depending on your conduct, how your credit history and payment patterns, and how credit-scoring technologies change.

Because the score is based on information in your credit history, it is very important that you review the credit related information that is being furnished to make sure it is accurate. Credit records may vary from one company to another.

If you have questions about your credit score or the credit information that is furnished to you, contact the credit bureau at the address and telephone number provided with this notice, or contact the lender, if the lender developed or generated the credit score. The credit bureau plays no part in the decision to take any action on the loan application and is unable to provide you with specific reasons for the decision on a loan application.

If you have questions concerning the terms of the loans, contact the lender.

The credit bureau(s) listed below provided a credit score that was used in connection with your home loan application.

CREDIT BUREAU #1	CREDIT BUREAU #2	CREDIT BUREAU #3
Experian P.O. Box 2104 Allen, TX 75013 (P)888-397-3742	Equifax P.O. Box 740241 Atlanta, GA 30374-0241 (P)800-997-2493	Trans Union P.O. Box 1000 Chester, PA 19022 (P)800-888-4213

I/We have received a copy of this disclosure.

_____ _____
Applicant   Date

_____ _____
Applicant   Date

For Your Protection: Get a Home Inspection

Property Address _____

What the FHA Does for Buyers... and What We Don't Do

What we do: FHA helps people become homeowners by insuring mortgages for lenders. This allows lenders to offer mortgages to first-time buyers and others who may not qualify for conventional loans. Because the FHA insures the loan for the lender, the buyer pays only a very low down-payment.

What we don't do: FHA does not guarantee the value or condition of your potential new home. If you find problems with your new home after closing, we can not give or lend you money for repairs, and we can not buy the home back from you.

That's why it's so important for you, the buyer, to get an independent home inspection. Ask a qualified home inspector to inspect your potential new home and give you the information you need to make a wise decision.

Appraisals and Home Inspections are Different

As part of our job insuring the loan, we require that the lender conduct an FHA appraisal. An appraisal is different from a home inspection. Appraisals are for lenders; home inspections are for buyers. The lender does an appraisal for three reasons:
* to estimate the value of a house
* to make sure that the house meets FHA minimum property standards
* to make sure that the house is marketable

Appraisals are not home inspections.

Why a Buyer Needs a Home Inspection

A home inspection gives the buyer more detailed information than an appraisal-- information you need to make a wise decision. In a home inspection, a qualified inspector takes an in-depth, unbiased look at your potential new home to:
* evaluate the physical condition: structure, construction, and mechanical systems
* identify items that need to be repaired or replaced
* estimate the remaining useful life of the major systems, equipment, structure, and finishes

What Goes into a Home Inspection

A home inspection gives the buyer an impartial, physical evaluation of the overall condition of the home and items that need to be repaired or replaced. The inspection gives a detailed report on the condition of the structural components, exterior, roofing, plumbing, electrical, heating, insulation and ventilation, air conditioning, and interiors.

Be an Informed Buyer

It is your responsibility to be an informed buyer. Be sure that what you buy is satisfactory in every respect. You have the right to carefully examine your potential new home with a qualified home inspector. You may arrange to do so before signing your contract, or may do so after signing the contract as long as your contract states that the sale of the home depends on the inspection.

I understand the importance of getting an independent home inspection. I have thought about this before I signed a contract with the seller for a home.

X _____ X _____
Signature & Date   Signature & Date

Insurance Disclosure

Private Mortgage Insurance Authorization:

I/We hereby understand that should the terms and conditions of the mortgage for which we are applying require Private Mortgage Insurance, the Lender will make application for and purchase the appropriate coverage on our behalf and at our expense. I/We understand that any approval of our mortgage application will be conditioned upon obtaining an approval for Private Mortgage Insurance. If applicable, I/We are responsible for payment of the first year's annual premium due or an acceptable escrow at the time of closing, and will apply $1/12^{th}$ of the annual renewal premium in addition to my/our regular monthly payment to be escrowed by the "Lender" for payment of the renewal premiums as they are due, unless the total is financed into the loan.

Hazard Insurance Requirement:

I/We understand that as a condition of our loan approval, I/We are required to obtain a Hazard Insurance Policy in the full amount of the mortgage. SAMPLE MORTGAGE CO. encourages you to insure your home for its replacement cost. You must provide the original policy and a one year paid receipt to Sample Mortgage Co. five business days prior to closing. You must provide a policy. We cannot accept a binder. PLEASE HAVE YOUR INSURANCE AGENT CONTACT SAMPLE MORTGAGE COMPANY. OFFICE FOR THE PROPER MORTGAGEE CLAUSE.

Flood Insurance Disclosure Authorization:

If at any time during the term of the Mortgage the "Lender" determines that the property is located in an area of special flood hazards, the undersigned agrees to provide Flood Insurance covering the full amount of the mortgage. You must provide the original policy with one year paid receipt to the "Lender". PLEASE CONTACT YOUR MORTGAGE COMPANY. OFFICE FOR THE PROPER MORTGAGEE CLAUSE.

Borrower   Co-Borrower

_____   _____
Printed Name   Printed Name

_____   _____
Signature   Date   Signature   Date

Your Mortgage co. Representative

ILLINOIS HOUSING DEVELOPMENT AUTHORITY
PRIVATE MORTGAGE INSURANCE DISCLOSURE & ACKNOWLEDGMENT

The undersigned ("Mortgagor") is requesting a mortgage loan from the Illinois Housing Development Authority (the "Authority") with a loan-to-value ratio that is greater than 80%. This means that the *amount of the mortgage loan is greater than 80% of the sales price or original appraised value, whichever is lower*. The lower of the sales price or the appraised value is the **Original Value**.

The Mortgagor acknowledges that:

1. The Authority requires **private mortgage insurance** ("PMI") to be obtained for this loan.

2. The Authority requires **private mortgage insurance** to be maintained on this loan until such time as the **amount owed on the loan** (the "Outstanding Principal Balance") is at least 80% of the Original Value.

<u>Paragraphs 1 and 2 above *are* the PMI Requirement</u>

3. The private mortgage insurance may be cancelled when:

   a. The Outstanding Principal Balance has been **paid down** to an amount no greater than 80% of the Original Value. <u>**No new appraisals will be considered**</u>; and

   b. The loan payment history shows **no late payments** for the previous 12 month period, and no **delinquent payments whatsoever**.

4. Requests for release from the PMI Requirement and cancellation of PMI insurance must be made to the **loan servicer** (the organization to which payments are sent) in writing at the address where the payments are sent.

The initial loan servicer on this loan is expected to be:

LOAN ➡ _____
SERVICER　　_____
　　　　　　　　　_____

5. If PMI insurance is cancelled, any **PMI premium refund** is at the sole discretion of the PMI insurer.

6. You will be notified, no less than annually, of the address and phone number to contact to determine whether you are eligible to cancel your PMI insurance, and the conditions and procedures applicable.

I have read and understand the foregoing Acknowledgement:

_____　　　　　_____
Mortgagor　　　　　　　　　　　　　　　　Date

_____　　　　　_____
Mortgagor　　　　　　　　　　　　　　　　Date

THE HOUSING FINANCIAL DISCRIMINATION ACT OF 1977
FAIR LENDING NOTICE

DATE:

APPLICATION NO: 03070010

PROPERTY ADDRESS:

It is illegal to discriminate in the provisions of or in the availability of financial assistance because of the consideration of:

1. Trends, characteristics or conditions in the neighborhood or geographic area surrounding a housing accommodation, unless the financial institution can demonstrate in the particular case that such consideration is required to avoid an unsafe and unsound business practice; or

2. Race, color, religion, sex, marital status, national origin or ancestry.

It is illegal to consider the racial, ethnic, religious or national origin composition of a neighborhood or geographic area surrounding a housing accommodation or whether or not such composition is undergoing change, or is expected to undergo change, in appraising a housing accommodation or in determining whether or not, or under what terms and conditions, to provide financial assistance.

These provisions govern financial assistance for the purpose of the purchase, construction, rehabilitation or refinancing of a one-to-four unit family residence occupied by the owner and for the purpose of the home improvement of any one-to-four unit family residence.

If you have any questions about your rights, or if you wish to file a complaint, contact the management of this financial institution or the agency noted below :

I/we received a copy of this notice.

_____   _____
           Date   Date

NOTICE TO HOMEOWNER

Property Address : _____   File No.: _____

Assumption of HUD/FHA-Insured Mortgages
Release of Personal Liability

You are legally obligated to make the monthly payments required by your mortgage (deed of trust) and promissory note.

The Department of Housing and Urban Development (HUD) has acted to keep investors and noncreditworthy purchasers from acquiring one- to four-family residential properties covered by certain FHA-insured mortgages. There are minor exceptions to the restriction on investors: loans to public agencies and some nonprofit organizations, Indian tribes or servicepersons; and loans under special mortgage insurance programs for property sold by HUD, rehabilitation loans or refinancing of insured mortgages. Your lender can advise you if you are included in one of these exceptions.

HUD will therefore direct the lender to accelerate this FHA-insured mortgage loan if all or part of the property is sold or transferred to a purchaser or recipient (1) who will not occupy the property as his or her principal residence, or (2) who does occupy the property but whose credit has not been approved in accordance with HUD requirements. This policy will apply except for certain sales or transfers where acceleration is prohibited by law.

When a loan is accelerated, the entire balance is declared "immediately due and payable." Since HUD will not approve the sale of the property covered by this mortgage to an investor or to a person whose credit has not been approved, you, the original homeowner, would remain liable for the mortgage debt even though the title to the property might have been transferred to the new buyer.

Even if you sell your home by letting an approved purchaser (that is, a creditworthy owner-occupant) assume your mortgage, you are still liable for the mortgage debt unless you obtain a release from liability from your mortgage lender. FHA-approved lenders have been instructed by HUD to prepare such a release when an original homeowner sells his or her property to a creditworthy purchaser who executes an agreement to assume and pay the mortgage debt and thereby agrees to become the substitute mortgagor. The release is contained in Form HUD-92210-1, ("Approval of Purchaser and Release of Seller"). You should ask for it if the mortgage lender does not provide it to you automatically when you sell your home to a creditworthy owner-occupant purchaser who executes an agreement to assume personal liability for the debt. When this form is executed, you are no longer liable for the mortgage debt.

You must sign and date this notice as indicated, return one copy to your lender as proof of notification and keep one copy for your records.

_____   _____
Applicant   Date

_____   _____
Applicant   Date

* Instruction to lender : A copy of this notice must be given to the mortgagor(s) on or before the date of settlement. You should retain asigned copy in the origination file.

HUD APPRAISED VALUE DISCLOSURE

Borrower(s):

Lender:

Property Address:

Loan Number:

I (We) understand that my (our) application for a FHA-insured mortgage is being requested under the Direct Endorsement (DE) program. The Lender has advised me (us) that the appraiser has assigned a value of $_____ to the property being purchased. I am (We are) aware that the final determination of value for mortgage insurance purposes will be made by the DE underwriter after he/she reviews the report. It is understood that I (we) may elect to cancel the application or renegotiate with the seller if the DE Underwriter reduces the value below the amount set forth in the sales contract or requires additional repairs for which the seller will not be responsible.

_____ _____   _____ _____
Borrower   Date   Borrower   Date

_____ _____   _____ _____
Borrower   Date   Borrower   Date

ALLIANCE HOME MORTGAGE, INC.
COMPLIANCE NOTICES

EQUAL CREDIT OPPORTUNITY ACT

The Federal Equal Opportunity Act prohibits creditors from discriminating against credit applicants on the basis of race, color, religion, national origin, sex, marital status, age (provided that the applicant has the capacity to enter into a binding contract); because all or part of the applicant's income derives from any public assistance program; or because the applicant has in good faith exercised any right under the Consumer Credit Protection Act. The federal agency that administers compliance with this law concerning this Mortgage Banker is the Federal Trade Commission located in Atlanta, Georgia 30308. The telephone number there is (404) 881-4836.

ANTI-COERCION STATEMENT

The insurance laws of this state provide that the lender may not require the applicant to take insurance through any particular agent or company to protect the mortgaged property. The applicant, Subject to the rules adopted by the Insurance Commissioner, has the right to have insurance placed with an insurance agent or company of his choice. Provided the company meets the requirements of the lender. The lender has the right to designate reasonable financial requirements as to the company and the adequacy of the coverage. I have read the foregoing statement, on the rules of the Insurance Commissioner relative thereto, and understand my rights and privileges and those of the lender relative to the placing of such insurance.

FLOOD INSURANCE NOTIFICATION

I acknowledge that I have been advised that flood insurance may or may not be required on the above-described property. I understand that I will be required to purchase a flood insurance policy prior to loan closing if the property is located in a flood area.

HOME BUYERS GUIDE TO SETTLEMENT COSTS

The undersigned applicant(s) certify that they have been furnished with the "Settlement Costs" A HUD Guide on this date.

ACKNOWLEDGEMENT OF RECEIPT OF CONSUMER HANDBOOK ON ADJUSTABLE RATE MORTGAGES

In accordance with Federal Home Loan Bank Board regulations, I/We hereby acknowledge receipt of the booklet "Consumer Handbook on Adjustable Rate Mortgages" which was presented to me/us along with the Residential Loan Application form.

APPRAISAL DISCLOSURE

On December 14, 1993 the Federal Reserve Board put into effect a rule which states that "creditors may automatically provide a copy of an appraisal report to all applicants for certain dwelling-secured loans, or they may provide a copy upon the applicant's request. Applicants may obtain a copy of the appraisal report by submitting a written request within 90 days of the loan application date. The applicant may be charged for copies. The lender has less than 30 days from receipt of the request to provide a copy of the appraisal report. **I/WE HEREBY CERTIFY THAT I/WE HAVE READ THE NOTICES SET FORTH ABOVE AND FULLY UNDERSTAND ALL OF THE ABOVE.**

APPLICANT_____ DATE_____

CO-APPLICANT_____ DATE_____

REQUEST

Notice Various Requests documents are sent out requesting vital information from companies such as, employment, banks, titles and others. This Requested information is need to prepare your files for underwriting and to close

Important: Your files will not close without the important information

Hint.. Make notes on the front cover of your file or envelope for reference and easy access to remind you of all your requests sent out and received

Example

Request sent out	**Date**
Verification Of Employment	_____
Verification Of Deposit	_____
Verification Of Rent (if renter)	_____
Ordered TITLE	_____
Ordered APPRAISAL	_____
Ordered HOME OWNER INSURANCE	_____

Request Received	**Date**
Verification Of Employment	_____
Verification Of Deposit	_____
Verification Of Rent (if renter)	_____
Ordered TITLE	_____
Ordered APPRAISAL	_____
Ordered HOME OWNER INSURANCE	_____

The Quicker you request the vital information and get it back in your file, the quicker your job is over and the file is closed..
The quicker your file is closed, the faster you get paid

No Closed files, No Money

Request for Verification of Loan

Privacy Act Notice: This information is to be used by the agency collecting it or its assignees in determining whether you qualify as a prospective mortgagor under its program. It will not be disclosed outside the agency except as required and permitted by law. You do not have to provide this information, but if you do not your application for approval as a prospective mortgagor or borrower may be delayed or rejected. This information requested in this form is authorized by Title 38, USC, Chapter 37 (if VA); by 12 USC, Section 1701 et seq. (if HUD/FHA); by 42 USC, Section 1452b (if HUD/CPD); and Title 42 USC, 1471 et. seq., or 7 USC, 1921 et. seq. (if USDA/FmHA).

Instructions: Lender - Complete items 1 through 8. Have applicant(s) complete item 9. Forward directly to creditor named in item 1.
Creditor - Please complete items 10 through 16 and return directly to lender named in item 2.
The form is to be transmitted directly to the lender and is not to be transmitted through the applicant(s) or any other party.

Lender's Phone No. 555-555-5555

Part I - Request

1. To (Name and address of creditor)
GMAC
PO Box 9874
Columbus, OH

2. From (Name and address of lender)

I certify that this information has been sent directly to the bank or creditor and has not passed through the hands of the applicant or any other interested party.

3. Signature of Lender	4. Title	5. Date	6. Lender's No. (Optional)
	Loan Officer	01/01/2002	

7. Information To Be Verified

Type of Loan	Loan in Name of	Loan Number	Balance
Auto Loan	John Doe	123456789	$14,000.00
			$
			$

To Creditor: We have applied for a mortgage loan and stated in my/our financial statement that the current loan balance with you is as shown above. You are authorized to verify this information and to supply the lender identified above with the information requested in items 10 through 11. Your response is solely a matter of courtesy for which no responsibility is attached to your institution or any of your officers.

8. Name and Address of Applicant(s)
John Doe, SSN: 123-45-6789
Jane Doe, SSN: 987-65-4321
567 Sunset Lane
Dallas, TX 75215

9. Signature of Applicant(s)
X SEE ATTACHMENT
X

To Be Completed by Creditor

Part II - Verification of Loan

10. Loan(s) Outstanding to Applicant(s)

Type of Loan	Loan Number	Date of Loan	Original Loan Amount	Secured by
			$	
			$	
			$	

Payments	Current Balance	Date last paid	Date next due	No. of late payments
$	$			
$	$			
$	$			

11. Please include any additional information which may be of assistance in determination of credit worthiness (Please include information on loans paid in full in item 10 above.)

Part III - Authorized Signature

Federal statutes provide severe penalties for any fraud, intentional misrepresentation, or criminal connivance or conspiracy purposed to influence the issuance of any guaranty or insurance by the VA Secretary, the U.S.D.A. FmHA/FHA Commissioner, or the HUD/CPD Assistant Secretary.

12. Signature of Creditor Representative	13. Title (Please print or type)	14. Date

15. Please print or type name signed in item 12	16. Phone No.

SAMPLE

Request for Verification of Employment

Privacy Act Notice: This information is to be used by the agency collecting it or its assignees in determining whether you qualify as a prospective mortgagor under its program. It will not be disclosed outside the agency except as required and permitted by law. You do not have to provide this information, but if you do not your application for approval as a prospective mortgagor or borrower may be delayed or rejected. The information requested in this form is authorized by Title 38, USC, Chapter 37 (if VA); by 12 USC, Section 1701 et. seq. (if HUD/FHA); by 42 USC, Section 1452b (if HUD/CPD) and Title 42 USC, 1471 et. seq., or 7 USC, 1921 et. seq. (if USDA/FmHA).

Instructions:
Lender – Complete items 1 through 7. Have applicant complete item 8. Forward directly to employer named in item 1.
Employer – Please complete either Part II or Part III as applicable. Complete Part IV and return directly to lender named in item 2.
The form is to be transmitted directly to the lender and is not to be transmitted through the applicant or any other party.

Part I — Request

1. To (Name and address of employer)	2. From (Name and address of lender)

I certify that this verification has been sent directly to the employer and has not passed through the hands of the applicant or any other interested party.

3. Signature of Lender	4. Title	5. Date	6. Lender's Number (Optional)

I have applied for a mortgage loan and stated that I am now or was formerly employed by you. My signature below authorizes verification of this information.

7. Name and Address of Applicant (include employee or badge number)	8. Signature of Applicant

Part II — Verification of Present Employment

9. Applicant's Date of Employment	10. Present Position	11. Probability of Continued Employment

12A. Current Gross Base Pay (Enter Amount and Check Period)
- ☐ Annual
- ☐ Hourly
- ☐ Monthly
- ☐ Other (Specify)
- ☐ Weekly

$ _____

13. For Military Personnel Only

Pay Grade	
Type	Monthly Amount
Base Pay	$
Rations	$
Flight or Hazard	$
Clothing	$
Quarters	$
Pro Pay	$
Overseas or Combat	$
Variable Housing Allowance	$

14. If Overtime or Bonus is Applicable, is its Continuance Likely?
Overtime ☐ Yes ☐ No
Bonus ☐ Yes ☐ No

15. If paid hourly – average hours per week

16. Date of applicant's next pay increase

17. Projected amount of next pay increase

18. Date of applicant's last pay increase

19. Amount of last pay increase

12B. Gross Earnings

Type	Year To Date Thru ____	Past Year	Past Year
Base Pay	$	$	$
Overtime	$	$	$
Commissions	$	$	$
Bonus	$	$	$
Total	$ 0.00	$ 0.00	$ 0.00

20. Remarks (If employee was off work for any length of time, please indicate time period and reason)

Part III — Verification of Previous Employment

21. Date Hired	23. Salary/Wage at Termination Per (Year) (Month) (Week)
22. Date Terminated	Base _____ Overtime _____ Commissions _____ Bonus _____
24. Reason for Leaving	25. Position Held

Part IV — Authorized Signature

Federal statutes provide severe penalties for any fraud, intentional misrepresentation, or criminal connivance or conspiracy purposed to influence the issuance of any guaranty or insurance by the VA Secretary, the U.S.D.A., FmHA/FHA Commissioner, or the HUD/CPD Assistant Secretary.

26. Signature of Employer	27. Title (Please print or type)	28. Date
29. Print or type name signed in Item 26	30. Phone No.	

REQUEST FOR VERIFICATION OF DEPOSIT

INSTRUCTIONS:
APPLICANT - Complete items 1, sign item 9 and return to the Rural Housing Service (RHS) Field Office address noted in block 2.
PACKAGER OR LENDER - Complete items 1 through 8. Have applicant complete item 9. Forward directly to depository named in block 1.
DEPOSITORY - Please complete items 10 through 18 and return DIRECTLY to address noted in block 2.

This form is to be transmitted directly to the lender and is not to be transmitted through the applicant or any other party.

Part I – Request

1. To (Name and address of depository)	2. From (Name and address of lender or RHS Office)

I certify that this verification has been sent directly to the bank or depository and has not passed through the hands of the applicant or any other party. This also certifies that the U.S. Department of Agriculture, acting through RHS, has complied with the applicable provisions of Title XI, the Right to Financial Privacy Act of 1978, Public Law 95-630, in seeking financial information regarding the below named applicant.

3. Signature of Lender/Packager/RHS	4. Title	5. Date	6. Lender's No. (Optional)

7. Information To Be Verified

Type of Account	Account in Name of	Account Number	Balance
			$
			$
			$

To Depository: I have applied for financial assistance from the United States Department of Agriculture and stated in my financial statement that the balance on deposit with you is as shown above. You are authorized to verify this information and to supply the lender identified above with the information requested in items 10 through 13. Your response is solely a matter of courtesy for which no responsibility is attached to your institution or any of your officers.

8. Name and Address of Applicant	9. Signature of Applicant

Part II – Verification of Depository *(TO BE COMPLETED BY DEPOSITORY)*

10. Deposit Accounts of Applicants

Type of Account	Account Number	Current Balance	Average Balance For Previous Two Months	Date Opened
		$	$	
		$	$	
		$	$	

11. Loans Outstanding To Applicants

Loan Number	Date of Loan	Original Amount	Current Balance	Installments (Monthly/Quarterly)	Secured By	Number of Late Payments (Last 12 Months)
		$	$	$ per		
		$	$	$ per		
		$	$	$ per		

12. Please include any additional information which may be of assistance in determination of credit worthiness. (Please include information on loans paid-in-full in Item 11 above.)

13. If the names on the accounts differ from those listed in Item 7, please supply the names on accounts as reflected by your records.

Part III – Authorized Signature

Federal statutes provide severe civil and criminal penalties for any person who knowingly makes false or fraudulent statements or representations to a government agency or officer with the intention of influencing any action by such agency or officer.

14. Signature of Depository Representative	15. Title (Please print or type)	16. Date

17. Please print or type name signed in item 14	18. Phone No.

Public reporting burden for this collection of information is estimated to average 1 hour per response, including the time for reviewing instructions, searching existing data sources, gathering and maintaining the data needed, and completing and reviewing the collection of information. Send comments regarding this burden estimate or any other aspect of this collection of information, including suggestions for reducing this burden, to U.S. Department of Agriculture, Clearance Officer, OIRM, STOP 7602, 1400 Independence Avenue, S.W., Washington, D.C. 20250-7602. **Please DO NOT RETURN this form to this address.** Forward to the local USDA office only. You are not required to respond to this collection of information unless it displays a currently valid OMB control number.

Request for Evidence of Insurance

1. To (Name and address of Insurance company):	2. From (Name and address of lender): BETTY YOUR LENDING CO 111 JOHN ST BLOOMINGTON, NY 111111 (P)

☐ Signature of Lender	☐ Title PROCESSOR	☐ Lender's No.

(p)111-111-11111/(F) ☐☐☐-☐☐☐-☐☐☐☐

5. Date

7. Name and address of applicant: SAMPLE ONLY BORROWER, MR 1☐☐ JOHN ST JOHNSTOWN, NY 1☐☐☐☐

(H) S5S-S55-555S
(B) 000-000-00000

Part II - Property and Mortgage ation:

☐ Property Type: [ ] Detached	[ ] Attached	[ ] condo	[ ] PUD	[ ] CO-OP
☐ Loan Purpose: [ ] [ ] Purchase	[ ] Cash-Out Refi	1 Lien Pos [ ] No Cash-Out Refi	1 [ ] First	[ ] Second

10. Sales Price: $ 150,000	11. Replacement Value: $ 1☐☐,000.00	1☐ Loan Amount: S

13. Property Address:
1☐☐ JOHN ST JOHNSTOWN, NY 1☐☐☐☐ County: Schenectady

14. Legal Description:
SEE TITLE

16. Estimated Closing

15. Lender (or Mortgagee):

0☐/10/☐000

17. Type of Insurance:
[ ] Wind /Storm [ ] Hazard
[ ] Flood

18. Insurance Escrowed:
Yes
[ ]

19. Comments:

Request for Verification of Rent or Mortgage Account

Privacy Act Notice: This information is to be used by the agency collecting it or its assignees in determining whether you qualify as a prospective mortgagor under its program. It will not be disclosed outside the agency except as required and permitted by law. You do not have to provide this information, but if you do not your application for approval as a prospective mortgagor or borrower may be delayed or rejected. The information requested in this form is authorized by title 38, USC, Chapter 37 (if V.A.); by 12 USC, Section 1701 et. seq. (if HUD/FHA); by 42 USC, Section 1452b (if HUD/CPD); and title 42 USC, 1471 et. seq., or 7 USC, 1921 et. seq. (if USDA/FmHA).

Instructions: Lender - Complete items 1 through 8. Have applicant(s) complete item 9. Forward directly to creditor named in item 1.
Landlord/Creditor - Please complete items 10 through 18 and return directly to lender named in item 2.
The form is to be transmitted directly to the lender and is not to be transmitted through the applicant(s) or any other party.

Part I – Request

1. To (Name and address of landlord/creditor)

2. From (Name and address of lender)
Enter Company Name in Global Defaults
1□□ Any Street
This City, WA □□□□□
□□□-□□□-1□□□

I certify that this verification has been sent directly to the landlord/creditor and has not passed through the hands of the applicant or any other interested party.

3. Signature of Lender	4. Title	5. Date	6. Lender's No. (Optional)
	Processor	1/□1/□00□	

☐ Information To Be Verified

Property Address
1□□ Current Address
My Town, WA □□□□□

Account in the Name of
John H. Sample
☒ Mortgage ☐ Rental
☐ Land Contract

Account Number

I have applied for a mortgage loan. My signature below authorizes verification of mortgage or rent information.

8. Name and Address of Applicant(s)
John H. Sample
1□□ Current Address
My Town, WA □□□□□

9. Signature of Applicant(s)
X
X

Part II – To Be Completed by Landlord/Creditor

We have received an application for a loan from the above, to whom we understand you rent or have extended a loan. In addition to the information requested below please furnish us with any information you might have that will assist us in processing of the loan.

☐ Rental Account ☐ Mortgage Account or ☐ Land Contract

10. Tenant rented from _____ to _____
Amount of rent $ _____ per _____
Number of late payments _____ *
Is account satisfactory? ☐ Yes ☐ No

11. Date account opened _____
Original contract amount $ _____
Current account balance $ _____
Monthly payment P&I only $ _____
Payment with taxes & ins. $ _____
Is account current? ☐ Yes ☐ No
Was loan assumed? ☐ Yes ☐ No
Satisfactory account? ☐ Yes ☐ No

12. Interest Rate _____ %
☐ FIXED ☐ ARM
☐ FHA ☐ VA
☐ CONV ☐ OTHER _____
Next pay date _____
No. of late payments _____
No. of late charges _____ *
Owner of First Mortgage
☐ FNMA ☐ FHLMC ☐ Seller/Other

*Payment History for the previous 12 months must be provided in order to comply with secondary mortgage market requirements.

13. Additional information which may be of assistance in determination of credit worthiness

Part III – Authorized Signature

Federal statutes provide severe penalties for any fraud, intentional misrepresentation, or criminal connivance or conspiracy purposed to influence the issuance of any guaranty or insurance by the V.A. Secretary, the USDA, FmHA/FHA Commissioner, or the HUD/CPD Assistant Secretary.

14. Signature of Landlord/Creditor Representative	15. Title (Please print or type)	16. Date

17. Print or type name signed in Item 14

18. Phone No.

Request for Title Commitment

1. To (Name and address) Title Co

From (Name and Address)
BETTY
YOUR LENDING CO
111 JOHN ST
BLOOMINGTON, NY 111111

(P) 111-111-11111 /(F) 222-222-22222

3. Signature of Lender	4. Title	5. Date	6. Lender's No.
	PROCESSOR		

7. Name and address of applicant
SAMPLE ONLY BORROWER, MR
1 JOHN ST JOHNSTOWN, NY 1
(P) 555-555-5555
(F) 000-000-00000

(SSN) 1 - -   (DOB) 01/01/ 00

8. Occupancy Status
[ ] Primary Residence [ ] Second Home [ ] Investment Property

[ ] Purchase [ ] Cash-Out Refi [ ] No Cash-Out Refi

10. Sales Price: 1 0,000

11. Loan Amount: 135,000.00

12. Property Address
1 JOHN ST ___ JOHNSTOWN, NY 1
County : Schenectady

13. Legal Description
SEE TITLE

14. Home Owner's Name and Phone Number	15. Property Type
	[ ] Detached [ ] Attached [ ] Condo [ ] CO-OP [ ] PUD
16. Seller	17. Mortgagee

18. Attachment
[ ] Prior Title Policy [ ]
[ ] Title Insurance Requirements [ ] Survey
[ ] Contract

19. Type of Policy

20. Estimated Closing Date

21. Mail Away
[ ] Yes [ ] NO

GIFT LETTER

Applicant(s): SAMPLE ONLY BORROWER, MR   Loan Number:

MR. BORROWER

1☐☐ JOHN ST
JOHNSTOWN, NY 1☐☐S

I, __Mr. Good Guy__ do hereby certify the following:
(Donor)

(1) I have made a gift of $ __5,000.00__ to __Mr. Borrower__
                              (Amount)   (Recipient)
   Whose relationship is: _____Friend_____
                                    (Relationship)

(2) This gift is to be applied toward the purchase of the property located at:
   __1☐☐ JOHN ST JOHNSTOWN, NY 1☐☐☐__
   (Property Address)

(3) No repayment of the gift is expected or implied in the form of cash or by future services of the recipient.

(4) The funds given to the homebuyer were not made available to the donor from any person or entity with an interest in the sale of the property including the seller, real estate agent or broker, builder, loan officer, or any entity associated with them.

(5) The source of this gift is:
                              (Source)

Donor Signature __Mr. Good Guy__ Date __01/01/00☐__

Borrower's Signature __BORROWER, MR__

Borrower Signature Sample ONLY

Donor Name (Print or Type)   Borrower Signature __BORROWER, MR__

Donor Address

Donor Phone Number

WARNING: Our signatures above indicate that we fully understand that it is a Federal Crime punishable by fine, imprisonment, or both to knowingly make any false statement concerning any of the above facts as applicable under the provision of Title 1☐, United States Code, Section 101☐ and 101☐.

Attachments:
1. Evidence of Donor's Ability to Provide Funds.
☐ Evidence of Receipt of Transfer of Funds.

Request for Appraisal

1. To (Name and address of appraiser)

2. From (Name and address)
BETTY
YOUR LENDING CO 111 JOHN ST
BLOOMINGTON, NY mill (P) 111-111-11111 / (F) 222-222-22222

3. Signature of Lender   1. Title   5. Date   6. Lender

PROCESSOR

7. Name and address of applicant
SAMPLE ONLY BORROWER,
MR 1☐☐ JOHN ST JOHNSTOWN,
NY 1☐☐☐☐

(H) 555-555-5555

(B) 000-000-00000

8. Property Type Detached ☐ Attached ☐ Condo ☐ CO-OP ☐	9. Occupancy Status is Primary Residence ☐ Second Home ☐ Investment Property No. of Units ☐	☐ USDA /Rural Housing Service 10. Type of Loan ☐ Conventional ☐ IFHA	☐ First Mortgage ☐ Second Mortgage	1☐. Loan Purpose ☐ Purchase ☐ Cash-Out Refi ☐ No Cash -Out Refi ☐

13. Sales Price: 1 0,000   14. Estimated Value : $ 15. Loan Amount: $ 1⊤,000.00

16. Property Address:
1☐☐ JOHN ST
JOHNSTOWN, NY 12345
County: Schenectady

17. Legal Description   19. Title Company:

18. Escrow Company:

           21. Selling Agent

20. Listing Agent

---

22. Due Date :

23. Type of Appraisal: |___| Interior / Exterior (Full) |___| Exterior Only |___| Market Rent Analysis

24. Contact for entry, if not same as borrower:

25. Comments

Understanding the Appraisal

Understanding

The

Appraisal

APPRAISAL OF REAL PROPERTY

LOCATED AT:
384 Spring Valley
See Title Policy

FOR:
Mortgage Service
Drive North

AS OF:
08/04/1998

BY:
Mr. Appraiser
License # 000111

NOTICE TO APPLICANT OF RIGHT
TO RECEIVE COPY OF APPRAISAL REPORT

APPLICATION NO:

PROPERTY ADDRESS:

You have the right to receive a copy of the appraisal report to be obtained in connection with the loan for which you are applying, provided that you have paid for the appraisal.
If you would like a copy of the appraisal report, contact:

        FirstNet Mortgage
        1350 41st Avenue, Suite #200
        Capitola, CA 95010

_____   _____
(Applicant)   (Date)   (Applicant)   (Date)

_____   _____
(Applicant)   (Date)   (Applicant)   (Date)

Uniform Residential Appraisal Report

File #

The purpose of this summary appraisal report is to provide the lender/client with an accurate, and adequately supported, opinion of the market value of the subject property.

Property Address	City	State	Zip Code
Borrower	Owner of Public Record	County	
Legal Description			
Assessor's Parcel #	Tax Year	R.E. Taxes $	
Neighborhood Name	Map Reference	Census Tract	
Occupant ☐ Owner ☐ Tenant ☐ Vacant	Special Assessments $	PUD HOA $ ☐ per year ☐ per month	
Property Rights Appraised ☐ Fee Simple ☐ Leasehold ☐ Other (describe)			
Assignment Type ☐ Purchase Transaction ☐ Refinance Transaction ☐ Other (describe)			
Lender/Client	Address		

Is the subject property currently offered for sale or has it been offered for sale in the twelve months prior to the effective date of this appraisal? ☐ Yes ☐ No
Report data source(s) used, offering price(s), and date(s).

☐ I did ☐ did not analyze the contract for sale for the subject purchase transaction. Explain the results of the analysis of the contract for sale or why the analysis was not performed.

Contract Price $ Date of Contract   Is the property seller the owner of public record? ☐ Yes ☐ No   Data Source(s)
Is there any financial assistance (loan charges, sale concessions, gift or downpayment assistance, etc.) to be paid by any party on behalf of the borrower? ☐ Yes ☐ No
If Yes, report the total dollar amount and describe the items to be paid.

Note: Race and the racial composition of the neighborhood are not appraisal factors.

Neighborhood Characteristics	One-Unit Housing Trends	One-Unit Housing	Present Land Use %
Location ☐ Urban ☐ Suburban ☐ Rural	Property Values ☐ Increasing ☐ Stable ☐ Declining	PRICE $(000) AGE (yrs)	One-Unit % 2-4 Unit %
Built-Up ☐ Over 75% ☐ 25-75% ☐ Under 25%	Demand/Supply ☐ Shortage ☐ In Balance ☐ Over Supply	Low	Multi-Family %
Growth ☐ Rapid ☐ Stable ☐ Slow	Marketing Time ☐ Under 3 mths ☐ 3-6 mths ☐ Over 6 mths	High Pred.	Commercial % Other %

Neighborhood Boundaries

Neighborhood Description

Market Conditions (including support for the above conclusions)

Dimensions	Area	Shape	View

Specific Zoning Classification   Zoning Description
Zoning Compliance ☐ Legal ☐ Legal Nonconforming (Grandfathered Use) ☐ No Zoning ☐ Illegal (describe)
Is the highest and best use of the subject property as improved (or as proposed per plans and specifications) the present use? ☐ Yes ☐ No   If No, describe

Utilities   Public   Other (describe)   Public   Other (describe)   Off-site Improvements—Type   Public   Private
Electricity   Water   Street
Gas   Sanitary Sewer   Alley

FEMA Special Flood Hazard Area ☐ Yes ☐ No   FEMA Flood Zone   FEMA Map #   FEMA Map Date
Are the utilities and off-site improvements typical for the market area? ☐ Yes ☐ No   If No, describe
Are there any adverse site conditions or external factors (easements, encroachments, environmental conditions, land uses, etc.)? ☐ Yes ☐ No   If Yes, describe

General Description	Foundation	Exterior Description materials/condition	Interior materials/condition
Units ☐ One ☐ One with Accessory Unit	☐ Concrete Slab ☐ Crawl Space	Foundation Walls	Floors
# of Stories	☐ Full Basement ☐ Partial Basement	Exterior Walls	Walls
Type ☐ Det. ☐ Att. ☐ S-Det/End Unit	Basement Area sq. ft.	Roof Surface	Trim/Finish
☐ Existing ☐ Proposed ☐ Under Const.	Basement Finish %	Gutters & Downspouts	Bath Floor
Design (Style)	☐ Outside Entry/Exit ☐ Sump Pump	Window Type	Bath Wainscot
Year Built	Evidence of ☐ Infestation	Storm Sash/Insulated	Car Storage ☐ None
Effective Age (Yrs)	☐ Dampness ☐ Settlement	Screens	Driveway # of Cars
Attic ☐ None	Heating ☐ FWA ☐ HWBB ☐ Radiant	Amenities Woodstove(s) #	Driveway Surface
☐ Drop Stair ☐ Stairs	☐ Other Fuel	☐ Fireplace(s) # ☐ Fence	Garage # of Cars
☐ Floor ☐ Scuttle	Cooling ☐ Central Air Conditioning	☐ Patio/Deck ☐ Porch	Carport # of Cars
☐ Finished ☐ Heated	☐ Individual ☐ Other	☐ Pool ☐ Other	☐ Att. ☐ Det. ☐ Built-in

Appliances ☐ Refrigerator ☐ Range/Oven ☐ Dishwasher ☐ Disposal ☐ Microwave ☐ Washer/Dryer ☐ Other (describe)

Finished area above grade contains: Rooms   Bedrooms   Bath(s)   Square Feet of Gross Living Area Above Grade

Additional features (special energy efficient items, etc.)

Describe the condition of the property (including needed repairs, deterioration, renovations, remodeling, etc.).

Are there any physical deficiencies or adverse conditions that affect the livability, soundness, or structural integrity of the property? ☐ Yes ☐ No   If Yes, describe

Does the property generally conform to the neighborhood (functional utility, style, condition, use, construction, etc.)? ☐ Yes ☐ No   If No, describe

Uniform Residential Appraisal Report

File #

There are _____ comparable properties currently offered for sale in the subject neighborhood ranging in price from $ _____ to $ _____
There are _____ comparable sales in the subject neighborhood within the past twelve months ranging in sale price from $ _____ to $ _____

FEATURE	SUBJECT	COMPARABLE SALE # 1	COMPARABLE SALE # 2	COMPARABLE SALE # 3
Address				
Proximity to Subject				
Sale Price	$	$	$	$
Sale Price/Gross Liv. Area	$ sq. ft.	$ sq. ft.	$ sq. ft.	$ sq. ft.
Data Source(s)				
Verification Source(s)				
VALUE ADJUSTMENTS	DESCRIPTION	DESCRIPTION	+(-) $ Adjustment	DESCRIPTION	+(-) $ Adjustment	DESCRIPTION	+(-) $ Adjustment
Sale or Financing Concessions				
Date of Sale/Time				
Location				
Leasehold/Fee Simple				
Site				
View				
Design (Style)				
Quality of Construction				
Actual Age				
Condition				
Above Grade Room Count	Total Bdrms. Baths	Total Bdrms. Baths	Total Bdrms. Baths	Total Bdrms. Baths
Gross Living Area	sq. ft.	sq. ft.	sq. ft.	sq. ft.
Basement & Finished Rooms Below Grade				
Functional Utility				
Heating/Cooling				
Energy Efficient Items				
Garage/Carport				
Porch/Patio/Deck				
Net Adjustment (Total)		☐ + ☐ − $	☐ + ☐ − $	☐ + ☐ − $
Adjusted Sale Price of Comparables		Net Adj. % Gross Adj. % $	Net Adj. % Gross Adj. % $	Net Adj. % Gross Adj. % $

I ☐ did ☐ did not research the sale or transfer history of the subject property and comparable sales. If not, explain

My research ☐ did ☐ did not reveal any prior sales or transfers of the subject property for the three years prior to the effective date of this appraisal.
Data source(s)
My research ☐ did ☐ did not reveal any prior sales or transfers of the comparable sales for the year prior to the date of sale of the comparable sale.
Data source(s)
Report the results of the research and analysis of the prior sale or transfer history of the subject property and comparable sales (report additional prior sales on page 3).

ITEM	SUBJECT	COMPARABLE SALE # 1	COMPARABLE SALE # 2	COMPARABLE SALE # 3
Date of Prior Sale/Transfer				
Price of Prior Sale/Transfer				
Data Source(s)				
Effective Date of Data Source(s)				

Analysis of prior sale or transfer history of the subject property and comparable sales

Summary of Sales Comparison Approach

Indicated Value by Sales Comparison Approach $
Indicated Value by: Sales Comparison Approach $ _____ Cost Approach (if developed) $ _____ Income Approach (if developed) $ _____

This appraisal is made ☐ "as is", ☐ subject to completion per plans and specifications on the basis of a hypothetical condition that the improvements have been completed, ☐ subject to the following repairs or alterations on the basis of a hypothetical condition that the repairs or alterations have been completed, or ☐ subject to the

Uniform Residential Appraisal Report

File #

ADDITIONAL COMMENTS

COST APPROACH TO VALUE (not required by Fannie Mae)

Provide adequate information for the lender/client to replicate the below cost figures and calculations.
Support for the opinion of site value (summary of comparable land sales or other methods for estimating site value)

ESTIMATED ☐ REPRODUCTION OR ☐ REPLACEMENT COST NEW | OPINION OF SITE VALUE .... = $
Source of cost data | Dwelling   Sq. Ft. @ $ = $
Quality rating from cost service   Effective date of cost data | Sq. Ft. @ $ = $
Comments on Cost Approach (gross living area calculations, depreciation, etc.)
 | Garage/Carport   Sq. Ft. @ $ = $
 | Total Estimate of Cost-New   = $
 | Less   Physical | Functional | External
 | Depreciation   =$(   )
 | Depreciated Cost of Improvements................. =$
 | "As-is" Value of Site Improvements................. =$

Estimated Remaining Economic Life (HUD and VA only)   Years | Indicated Value By Cost Approach .... $

INCOME APPROACH TO VALUE (not required by Fannie Mae)

Estimated Monthly Market Rent $ X Gross Rent Multiplier   = $ Indicated Value by Income Approach
Summary of Income Approach (including support for market rent and GRM)

PROJECT INFORMATION FOR PUDs (if applicable)

Is the developer/builder in control of the Homeowners' Association (HOA)?   ☐ Yes   ☐ No   Unit type(s)   ☐ Detached   ☐ Attached

Provide the following information for PUDs ONLY if the developer/builder is in control of the HOA and the subject property is an attached dwelling unit.

Legal name of project
Total number of phases   Total number of units   Total number of units sold
Total number of units rented   Total number of units for sale   Data source(s)
Was the project created by the conversion of an existing building(s) into a PUD?   ☐ Yes   ☐ No   If Yes, date of conversion
Does the project contain any multi-dwelling units?   ☐ Yes   ☐ No   Data source(s)
Are the units, common elements, and recreation facilities complete? ☐ Yes   ☐ No   If No, describe the status of completion

Uniform Residential Appraisal Report

File #

This report form is designed to report an appraisal of a one-unit property or a one-unit property with an accessory unit; including a unit in a planned unit development (PUD). This report form is not designed to report an appraisal of a manufactured home or a unit in a condominium or cooperative project.

This appraisal report is subject to the following scope of work, intended use, intended user, definition of market value, statement of assumptions and limiting conditions, and certifications. Modifications, additions, or deletions to the intended use, intended user, definition of market value, or assumptions and limiting conditions are not permitted. The appraiser may expand the scope of work to include any additional research or analysis necessary based on the complexity of this appraisal assignment. Modifications or deletions to the certifications are also not permitted. However, additional certifications that do not constitute material alterations to this appraisal report, such as those required by law or those related to the appraiser's continuing education or membership in an appraisal organization, are permitted.

SCOPE OF WORK: The scope of work for this appraisal is defined by the complexity of this appraisal assignment and the reporting requirements of this appraisal report form, including the following definition of market value, statement of assumptions and limiting conditions, and certifications. The appraiser must, at a minimum: (1) perform a complete visual inspection of the interior and exterior areas of the subject property, (2) inspect the neighborhood, (3) inspect each of the comparable sales from at least the street, (4) research, verify, and analyze data from reliable public and/or private sources, and (5) report his or her analysis, opinions, and conclusions in this appraisal report.

INTENDED USE: The intended use of this appraisal report is for the lender/client to evaluate the property that is the subject of this appraisal for a mortgage finance transaction.

INTENDED USER: The intended user of this appraisal report is the lender/client.

DEFINITION OF MARKET VALUE: The most probable price which a property should bring in a competitive and open market under all conditions requisite to a fair sale, the buyer and seller, each acting prudently, knowledgeably and assuming the price is not affected by undue stimulus. Implicit in this definition is the consummation of a sale as of a specified date and the passing of title from seller to buyer under conditions whereby: (1) buyer and seller are typically motivated; (2) both parties are well informed or well advised, and each acting in what he or she considers his or her own best interest; (3) a reasonable time is allowed for exposure in the open market; (4) payment is made in terms of cash in U. S. dollars or in terms of financial arrangements comparable thereto; and (5) the price represents the normal consideration for the property sold unaffected by special or creative financing or sales concessions* granted by anyone associated with the sale.

*Adjustments to the comparables must be made for special or creative financing or sales concessions. No adjustments are necessary for those costs which are normally paid by sellers as a result of tradition or law in a market area; these costs are readily identifiable since the seller pays these costs in virtually all sales transactions. Special or creative financing adjustments can be made to the comparable property by comparisons to financing terms offered by a third party institutional lender that is not already involved in the property or transaction. Any adjustment should not be calculated on a mechanical dollar for dollar cost of the financing or concession but the dollar amount of any adjustment should approximate the market's reaction to the financing or concessions based on the appraiser's judgment.

STATEMENT OF ASSUMPTIONS AND LIMITING CONDITIONS: The appraiser's certification in this report is subject to the following assumptions and limiting conditions:

1. The appraiser will not be responsible for matters of a legal nature that affect either the property being appraised or the title to it, except for information that he or she became aware of during the research involved in performing this appraisal. The appraiser assumes that the title is good and marketable and will not render any opinions about the title.

2. The appraiser has provided a sketch in this appraisal report to show the approximate dimensions of the improvements. The sketch is included only to assist the reader in visualizing the property and understanding the appraiser's determination of its size.

3. The appraiser has examined the available flood maps that are provided by the Federal Emergency Management Agency (or other data sources) and has noted in this appraisal report whether any portion of the subject site is located in an identified Special Flood Hazard Area. Because the appraiser is not a surveyor, he or she makes no guarantees, express or implied, regarding this determination.

4. The appraiser will not give testimony or appear in court because he or she made an appraisal of the property in question, unless specific arrangements to do so have been made beforehand, or as otherwise required by law.

5. The appraiser has noted in this appraisal report any adverse conditions (such as needed repairs, deterioration, the presence of hazardous wastes, toxic substances, etc.) observed during the inspection of the subject property or that he or she became aware of during the research involved in performing this appraisal. Unless otherwise stated in this appraisal report, the appraiser has no knowledge of any hidden or unapparent physical deficiencies or adverse conditions of the property (such as, but not limited to, needed repairs, deterioration, the presence of hazardous wastes, toxic substances, adverse environmental conditions, etc.) that would make the property less valuable, and has assumed that there are no such conditions and makes no guarantees or warranties, express or implied. The appraiser will not be responsible for any such conditions that do exist or for any engineering or testing that might be required to discover whether such conditions exist. Because the appraiser is not an expert in the field of environmental hazards, this appraisal report must not be considered as an environmental assessment of the property.

6. The appraiser has based his or her appraisal report and valuation conclusion for an appraisal that is subject to satisfactory completion, repairs, or alterations on the assumption that the completion, repairs, or alterations of the subject property will be performed in a professional manner.

Uniform Residential Appraisal Report   File #

APPRAISER'S CERTIFICATION: The Appraiser certifies and agrees that:

1. I have, at a minimum, developed and reported this appraisal in accordance with the scope of work requirements stated in this appraisal report.

2. I performed a complete visual inspection of the interior and exterior areas of the subject property. I reported the condition of the improvements in factual, specific terms. I identified and reported the physical deficiencies that could affect the livability, soundness, or structural integrity of the property.

3. I performed this appraisal in accordance with the requirements of the Uniform Standards of Professional Appraisal Practice that were adopted and promulgated by the Appraisal Standards Board of The Appraisal Foundation and that were in place at the time this appraisal report was prepared.

4. I developed my opinion of the market value of the real property that is the subject of this report based on the sales comparison approach to value. I have adequate comparable market data to develop a reliable sales comparison approach for this appraisal assignment. I further certify that I considered the cost and income approaches to value but did not develop them, unless otherwise indicated in this report.

5. I researched, verified, analyzed, and reported on any current agreement for sale for the subject property, any offering for sale of the subject property in the twelve months prior to the effective date of this appraisal, and the prior sales of the subject property for a minimum of three years prior to the effective date of this appraisal, unless otherwise indicated in this report.

6. I researched, verified, analyzed, and reported on the prior sales of the comparable sales for a minimum of one year prior to the date of sale of the comparable sale, unless otherwise indicated in this report.

7. I selected and used comparable sales that are locationally, physically, and functionally the most similar to the subject property.

8. I have not used comparable sales that were the result of combining a land sale with the contract purchase price of a home that has been built or will be built on the land.

9. I have reported adjustments to the comparable sales that reflect the market's reaction to the differences between the subject property and the comparable sales.

10. I verified, from a disinterested source, all information in this report that was provided by parties who have a financial interest in the sale or financing of the subject property.

11. I have knowledge and experience in appraising this type of property in this market area.

12. I am aware of, and have access to, the necessary and appropriate public and private data sources, such as multiple listing services, tax assessment records, public land records and other such data sources for the area in which the property is located.

13. I obtained the information, estimates, and opinions furnished by other parties and expressed in this appraisal report from reliable sources that I believe to be true and correct.

14. I have taken into consideration the factors that have an impact on value with respect to the subject neighborhood, subject property, and the proximity of the subject property to adverse influences in the development of my opinion of market value. I have noted in this appraisal report any adverse conditions (such as, but not limited to, needed repairs, deterioration, the presence of hazardous wastes, toxic substances, adverse environmental conditions, etc.) observed during the inspection of the subject property or that I became aware of during the research involved in performing this appraisal. I have considered these adverse conditions in my analysis of the property value, and have reported on the effect of the conditions on the value and marketability of the subject property.

15. I have not knowingly withheld any significant information from this appraisal report and, to the best of my knowledge, all statements and information in this appraisal report are true and correct.

16. I stated in this appraisal report my own personal, unbiased, and professional analysis, opinions, and conclusions, which are subject only to the assumptions and limiting conditions in this appraisal report.

17. I have no present or prospective interest in the property that is the subject of this report, and I have no present or prospective personal interest or bias with respect to the participants in the transaction. I did not base, either partially or completely, my analysis and/or opinion of market value in this appraisal report on the race, color, religion, sex, age, marital status, handicap, familial status, or national origin of either the prospective owners or occupants of the subject property or of the present owners or occupants of the properties in the vicinity of the subject property or on any other basis prohibited by law.

18. My employment and/or compensation for performing this appraisal or any future or anticipated appraisals was not conditioned on any agreement or understanding, written or otherwise, that I would report (or present analysis supporting) a predetermined specific value, a predetermined minimum value, a range or direction in value, a value that favors the cause of any party, or the attainment of a specific result or occurrence of a specific subsequent event (such as approval of a pending mortgage loan application).

19. I personally prepared all conclusions and opinions about the real estate that were set forth in this appraisal report. If I relied on significant real property appraisal assistance from any individual or individuals in the performance of this appraisal or the preparation of this appraisal report, I have named such individual(s) and disclosed the specific tasks performed in this appraisal report. I certify that any individual so named is qualified to perform the tasks. I have not authorized anyone to make a change to any item in this appraisal report; therefore, any change made to this appraisal is unauthorized and I will take no responsibility for it.

20. I identified the lender/client in this appraisal report who is the individual, organization, or agent for the organization that ordered and will receive this appraisal report.

Uniform Residential Appraisal Report   File #

21. The lender/client may disclose or distribute this appraisal report to: the borrower; another lender at the request of the borrower; the mortgagee or its successors and assigns; mortgage insurers; government sponsored enterprises; other secondary market participants; data collection or reporting services; professional appraisal organizations; any department, agency, or instrumentality of the United States; and any state, the District of Columbia, or other jurisdictions; without having to obtain the appraiser's or supervisory appraiser's (if applicable) consent. Such consent must be obtained before this appraisal report may be disclosed or distributed to any other party (including, but not limited to, the public through advertising, public relations, news, sales, or other media).

22. I am aware that any disclosure or distribution of this appraisal report by me or the lender/client may be subject to certain laws and regulations. Further, I am also subject to the provisions of the Uniform Standards of Professional Appraisal Practice that pertain to disclosure or distribution by me.

23. The borrower, another lender at the request of the borrower, the mortgagee or its successors and assigns, mortgage insurers, government sponsored enterprises, and other secondary market participants may rely on this appraisal report as part of any mortgage finance transaction that involves any one or more of these parties.

24. If this appraisal report was transmitted as an "electronic record" containing my "electronic signature," as those terms are defined in applicable federal and/or state laws (excluding audio and video recordings), or a facsimile transmission of this appraisal report containing a copy or representation of my signature, the appraisal report shall be as effective, enforceable and valid as if a paper version of this appraisal report were delivered containing my original hand written signature.

25. Any intentional or negligent misrepresentation(s) contained in this appraisal report may result in civil liability and/or criminal penalties including, but not limited to, fine or imprisonment or both under the provisions of Title 18, United States Code, Section 1001, et seq., or similar state laws.

SUPERVISORY APPRAISER'S CERTIFICATION: The Supervisory Appraiser certifies and agrees that:

1. I directly supervised the appraiser for this appraisal assignment, have read the appraisal report, and agree with the appraiser's analysis, opinions, statements, conclusions, and the appraiser's certification.

2. I accept full responsibility for the contents of this appraisal report including, but not limited to, the appraiser's analysis, opinions, statements, conclusions, and the appraiser's certification.

3. The appraiser identified in this appraisal report is either a sub-contractor or an employee of the supervisory appraiser (or the appraisal firm), is qualified to perform this appraisal, and is acceptable to perform this appraisal under the applicable state law.

4. This appraisal report complies with the Uniform Standards of Professional Appraisal Practice that were adopted and promulgated by the Appraisal Standards Board of The Appraisal Foundation and that were in place at the time this appraisal report was prepared.

5. If this appraisal report was transmitted as an "electronic record" containing my "electronic signature," as those terms are defined in applicable federal and/or state laws (excluding audio and video recordings), or a facsimile transmission of this appraisal report containing a copy or representation of my signature, the appraisal report shall be as effective, enforceable and valid as if a paper version of this appraisal report were delivered containing my original hand written signature.

APPRAISER
Signature _____
Name _____
Company Name _____
Company Address _____

Telephone Number _____
Email Address _____
Date of Signature and Report _____
Effective Date of Appraisal _____
State Certification # _____ or
State License # _____ or
Other (describe) _____ State # _____
State _____
Expiration Date of Certification or License _____

ADDRESS OF PROPERTY APPRAISED
_____
_____

APPRAISED VALUE OF SUBJECT PROPERTY $ _____
LENDER/CLIENT
Name _____
Company Name _____
Company Address _____

Email Address _____

SUPERVISORY APPRAISER (ONLY IF REQUIRED)
Signature _____
Name _____
Company Name _____
Company Address _____

Telephone Number _____
Email Address _____
Date of Signature _____
State Certification # _____
or State License # _____
State _____
Expiration Date of Certification or License _____

SUBJECT PROPERTY

☐ Did not inspect subject property
☐ Did inspect exterior of subject property from street
    Date of Inspection _____
☐ Did inspect interior and exterior of subject property
    Date of Inspection _____

COMPARABLE SALES

☐ Did not inspect exterior of comparable sales from street
☐ Did inspect exterior of comparable sales from street
    Date of Inspection _____

Statement of Limiting Conditions and Apraiser's Certification

DEFINITION OF MARKET VALUE: The most probable price which a property should bring in a competitive and open market under all conditions requisite to a fair sale, the buyer and seller, each acting prudently, knowledgeably and assuming the price is not affected by undue stimulus. Implicit in this definition is the consummation of a sale as of a specified date and the passing of title from seller to buyer under conditions whereby: (1) buyer and seller are typically motivated; (2) both parties are well informed or well advised, and each acting in what he considers his own best interest; (3) a reasonable time is allowed for exposure in the open market; (4) payment is made in terms of cash in U. S. dollars or in terms of financial arrangements comparable thereto; and (5) the price represents the normal consideration for the property sold unaffected by special or creative financing or sales concessions* granted by anyone associated with the sale.

*Adjustments to the comparables must be made for special or creative financing or sales concessions. No adjustments are necessary for those costs which are normally paid by sellers as a result of tradition or law in a market area; these costs are readily identifiable since the seller pays these costs in virtually all sales transactions. Special or creative financing adjustments can be made to the comparable property by comparisons to financing terms offered by a third Party institutional lender that is not already involved in the property or transaction. Any adjustment should not be calculated on a mechanical dollar for dollar cost of the financing or concession but the dollar amount of any adjustment. should approximate the market's reaction to the financing or concessions based on the appraiser's judgment.

STATEMENT OF LIMITING CONDITIONS AND APPRAISER'S CERTIFICATION

CONTINGENT AND LIMITING CONDITIONS: The appraiser's certification that appears in the appraisal report is subject to the following conditions:

1. The appraiser will not be responsible for matters of a legal nature that affect either the property being appraised or the title to it. The appraiser assumes that the title is good and marketable and, therefore, will not render any opinions about the title. The property is appraised on the basis of it being under responsible ownership.

2. The appraiser has provided a sketch in the appraisal report to show approximate dimensions of the improvements and the sketch is included only to assist the reader of the report in visualizing the property and understanding the appraiser's determination of its size.

3. The appraiser has examined the available flood maps that are provided by the Federal Emergency Management Agency (or other data sources) and has noted in the appraisal report whether the subject site is located in an identified Special Flood Hazard Area. Because the appraiser is not a surveyor, he or she makes no guarantees, express or implied, regarding this determination.

4. The appraiser will not give testimony or appear in court because he or she made an appraisal of the property in question, unless specific arrangements to do so have been made beforehand.

5. The appraiser has estimated the value of the land in the cost approach at its highest and best use and the improvements at their contributory value. These separate valuations of the land and improvements must not be used in conjunction with any other appraisal and are invalid if they are so used.

6. The appraiser has noted in the appraisal report any adverse conditions (such as, needed repairs, depreciation, the presence of hazardous wastes, toxic substances, etc.) observed during the inspection of the subject property or that he or she became aware of during the normal research involved in performing the appraisal. Unless otherwise stated in the appraisal report, the appraiser has no knowledge of any hidden or unapparent conditions of the property or adverse environmental conditions (including the presence of hazardous wastes, toxic substances, etc.) that would make the property more or less valuable, and has assumed that there are no such conditions and makes no guarantees or warranties, express or implied, regarding the condition of the property. The appraiser will not be responsible for any such conditions that do exist or for any engineering or testing that might be required to discover whether such conditions exist. Because the appraiser is not an expert in the field of environmental hazards, the appraisal report must not be considered as an environmental assessment of the property.

7. The appraiser obtained the information, estimates, and opinions that were expressed in the appraisal report from sources that he or she considers to be reliable and believes them to be true and correct. The appraiser does not assume responsibility for the accuracy of such items that were furnished by other parties.

8. The appraiser will not disclose the contents of the appraisal report except as provided for in the Uniform Standards of Professional Appraisal Practice.

9. The appraiser has based his or her appraisal report and valuation conclusion for an appraisal that is subject to satisfactory completion, repairs, or alterations on the assumption that completion of the improvements will be performed in a workmanlike manner.

10. The appraiser must provide his or her prior written consent before the lender/client, specified in the appraisal report can distribute the appraisal report (including conclusions about the property value, the appraiser's identity and professional designations, and references to any professional appraisal organizations or the firm with which the appraiser is associated) to anyone other than the borrower; the mortgagee or its successors and assigns; the mortgage insurer; consultants; professional appraisal organizations; any state or federally approved financial institution; or any department, agency, or instrumentality of the United States or any state or the District of Columbia; except that the lender/client may distribute the property description section of the report only to data collection or reporting service(s) without, having to obtain the appraiser's prior written consent. The appraiser's written consent and approval must also be obtained before the appraisal can be conveyed by anyone to the public through advertising, public relations, news, sales, or other media.

APPRAISER'S CERTIFICATION: The Appraiser certifies and agrees that:

1. I have researched the subject market area and have selected a minimum of three recent sales of properties most Similar and Proximate to the subject property for consideration in the sales comparison analysis and have made a dollar adjustment when appropriate to reflect the market reaction to those items of significant variation. If a significant item in a comparable property is superior to, or more favorable than, the subject property, I have made a negative adjustment to reduce the adjusted sales price of the comparable and, if a significant item in a comparable property is inferior to, or less favorable than the subject property, I have made a positive adjustment to increase the adjusted sales price of the comparable.

2. I have taken into consideration the factors that have an impact on value in my development of the estimate of market value in the appraisal report. I have not knowingly withheld any significant information from the appraisal report and I believe, to the best of my knowledge, that all statements and information in the appraisal report are true and correct.

3. I stated in the appraisal report only my own personal, unbiased, and professional analysis, opinions, and conclusions, which are subject only to the contingent and limiting conditions specified in this form.

4. I have no present or prospective interest in the property that is the subject to this report, and I have no present or prospective personal interest or bias with respect to the participants in the transaction. I did not base, either partially or completely, my analysis and/or the estimate of market value in the appraisal report on the race, color, religion, sex, handicap, familial status, or national origin of either the prospective owners or occupants of the subject property or of the present owners or occupants of the properties in the vicinity of the subject property.

5. I have no present or contemplated future interest in the subject property, and neither my current or future employment nor my compensation for performing this appraisal is contingent on the appraised value of the property.

6. I was not required to report a predetermined value or direction in value that favors the cause of the client or any related party, the amount of the value estimate, the attainment of a specific result, or the occurrence of a subsequent event in order to receive my compensation and/or employment for performing the appraisal. I did not base the appraisal report on a requested minimum valuation, a specific valuation, or the need to approve a specific mortgage loan.

7. I performed this appraisal in conformity with the Uniform Standards of Professional Appraisal Practice that were adopted and promulgated by the Appraisal Standards Board of the Appraisal Foundation and that were in place as of the effective date of this appraisal, with the exception of the departure provision of those Standards, which does not apply. I acknowledge that an estimate of a reasonable time for exposure in the open market is a condition in the definition of market value and the estimate I developed is consistent with the marketing time noted in the neighborhood section of this report, unless I have otherwise stated in the reconciliation section.

8. I have personally inspected the interior and exterior areas of the subject property and the exterior of all properties listed as comparables in the appraisal report. I further certify that I have noted any apparent or known adverse conditions in the subject improvements, on the subject site, or on any site within the immediate vicinity of the subject property of which I am aware and have made adjustments for these adverse conditions in my analysis of the property value to the extent that I had market evidence to support them. I have also commented about the effect of the adverse conditions on the marketability of the subject property.

9. I personally prepared all conclusions and opinions about the real estate that were set forth in the appraisal report. If I relied on significant professional assistance from any individual or individuals in the performance of the appraisal or the preparation of the appraisal report, I have named such individual(s) and disclosed the specific tasks performed by them in the reconciliation section of this appraisal report. I certify that any individual so named is qualified to perform the tasks. I have not authorized anyone to make a change to any item in the report; therefore, if an unauthorized change is made to the appraisal report, I will take no responsibility for it.

SUPERVISORY APPRAISER'S CERTIFICATION: If a supervisory appraiser signed the appraisal report, he or she certifies and agrees that: I directly supervise the appraiser who prepared the appraisal report, have reviewed the appraisal report, agree with the statements and conclusions of the appraiser, agree to be bound by the appraiser's certifications numbered 4 through 7 above, and am taking full responsibility for the appraisal and the appraisal report.

ADDRESS OF PROPERTY
APPRAISED: _____ APPRAISER: _____

	SUPERVISORY APPRAISER (only if required):
Signature: _____	Signature: _____
Name: _____	Name: _____
Date Signed: _____	Date Signed: _____
State Certification #: _____	State Certification #: _____ or
State License #: _____	or State License #: _____
State: _____	State: _____
Expiration Date of Certification or License: _____	Expiration Date of Certification or License: _____

☐ Did   ☐ Did Not Inspect Property

HUD APPRAISED VALUE DISCLOSURE

Borrower(s):

Lender:

Property Address:

Loan Number:

I (We) understand that my (our) application for a FHA-insured mortgage is being requested under the Direct Endorsement (DE) program. The Lender has advised me (us) that the appraiser has assigned a value of $_____ to the property being purchased. I am (We are) aware that the final determination of value for mortgage insurance purposes will be made by the DE underwriter after he/she reviews the report. It is understood that I (we) may elect to cancel the application or renegotiate with the seller if the DE Underwriter reduces the value below the amount set forth in the sales contract or requires additional repairs for which the seller will not be responsible.

_____ _____   _____ _____
Borrower   Date   Borrower   Date

_____ _____   _____ _____
Borrower   Date   Borrower   Date

Subject Photo Page (1 of 5)

Borrower/Client	Mr. Borrower			
Property Address	384 Spring Valley			
City	In USA	County	In USA	State In USA	Zip Code 00000
Lender	Fictitious Lender : **For Viewing Sample only**

Subject Front

Sales Price 399,990.00
Gross Living Area 2600
Total Rooms 9
Total Bedrooms 4
Total Bathrooms 2.5
Location IL.
View Lake
Site 1.5 Acres
Quality Brick
Age New

Subject Rear

Subject Street

SAMPLE SOLELY FOR VIEWING PURPOSES @ www.2-appraise.com- ALTERATIONS STRICTLY PROHIBITED

Comparable Photo Page

Borrower/Client	Mr. Borrower					
Property Address	In IL.					
City	In IL.	County	In IL.	State	In IL.	Zip Code 00000
Lender	Your Lender	For Viewing Purposes only				

Comparable 1

Prox. to Subject	0.20 miles
Sale Price	459,000.00
Gross Living Area	3400
Total Rooms	10
Total Bedrooms	4
Total Bathrooms	3
Location	IL.
View	Open Space
Site	1.5 Acres
Quality	Brick
Age	New

Comparable 2

Prox. to Subject	0.13 miles
Sale Price	350,000.00
Gross Living Area	2600
Total Rooms	8
Total Bedrooms	4
Total Bathrooms	2.5
Location	IL.
View	
Site	1.5 Acres
Quality	Brick
Age	New

Comparable 3

3126 SW 65th Street

Prox. to Subject	0.13 miles
Sale Price	
Gross Living Area	3,295
Total Rooms	12
Total Bedrooms	4
Total Bathrooms	2.5
Location	IL.
View	Open
Site	1.5 Acres
Quality	Brick
Age	New

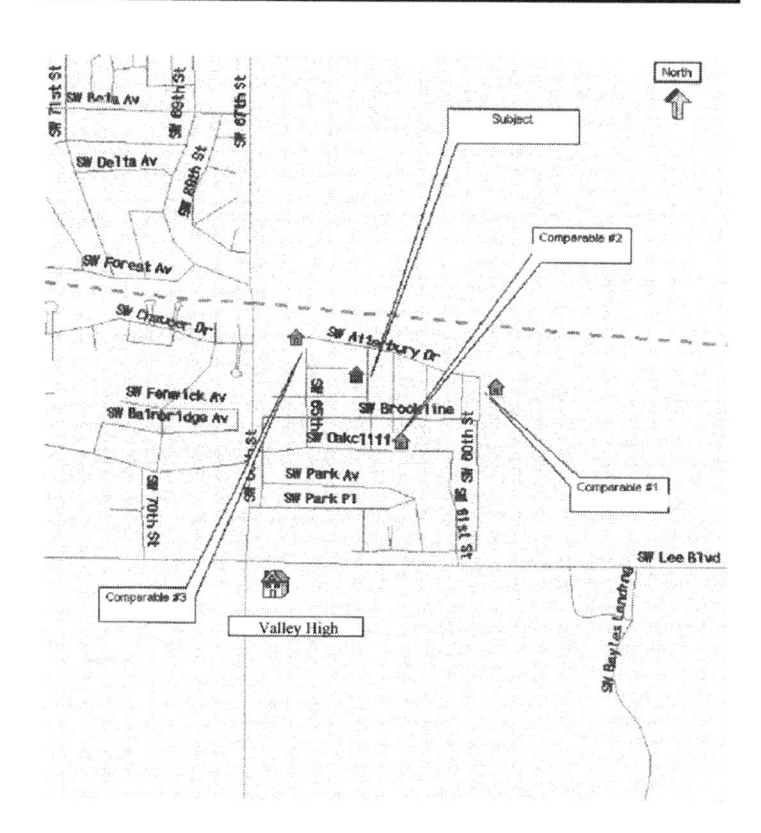

Glossary

Mortgage Glossary

Acceleration clause: A clause in your mortgage that allows the lender to demand payment of the outstanding loan balance for various reasons. The most common reasons for accelerating a loan are if the borrower defaults on the loan or transfers title to another individual without informing the lender.

Adjustable -rate mortgage (ARM)
Is a mortgage in which the interest rate is adjusted periodically based on a pre-selected index, also sometimes known as the re negotiable rate mortgage, the variable rate mortgage or the Canadian rollover mortgage.

Adjustment date: the date on which the interest rate changes for an adjustable-rate mortgage (ARM). Adjustment Period: the period that elapses between the adjustment dates for an adjustable-rate mortgage (ARM).

Amortization: the repayment of a mortgage loan by installments with regular payments to cover the principal and interest.

Amortization term: The amount of time required to amortize the mortgage loan. The amortization term is expressed as a number of months. For example, for a 30-year fixed-rate mortgage, the amortization term is 360 months.

Annual percentage rate (APR): A tool used to compare bans across different lenders. The cost of a mortgage stated as a yearly rate; includes such items as interest, mortgage insurance, and loan origination fee (points) The true cost of the loan to the borrower expressed in the form of a yearly rate. The Federal Truth in lending law requires mortgage companies to disclose the APR when they advertise a rate.

Application: A form, commonly referred to as a 1003 form, used to apply for a mortgage and to provide information regarding a prospective mortgagor and the proposed security mortgage stated as a yearly rate; includes such items as interest, mortgage insurance, and loan Origination fee (points).

Appraisal: a written analysis of the estimated value of a property prepared by a qualified appraiser.
Appraiser: A person qualified by education, training, and experience to estimate the value of real property and personal property.

Appreciation: an increase in the value of a property due to changes in market conditions or other causes: The opposite of depreciation.

Assessed value: The valuation placed on property by a public tax assessor for purposes of taxation.

Assessment: The process of placing a value on property for the strict purpose of taxation. May also refer to a levy against property for a special purpose such as sewer assessment.

Asset: anything of monetary value that is owned by a person. Assets include real property, personal property, and enforceable claims against others (including bank accounts, stocks, mutual funds, and so on).

Assignment: the transfer of a mortgage from one person to another.

Assumable mortgage: a mortgage that can be taken over ("assumed") by the buyer when a home is sold...

Assumption: the transfer of the seller's existing mortgage to the buyer

Assumption clause: A provision in an assumable mortgage that allows a buyer to assume responsibility for the mortgage from the seller. The loan does not need to be paid in full by the original borrower upon sale or transfer of the property

Assumption fee: The fee paid to a lender (usually by the purchaser of real property) resulting from the assumption of an existing mortgage, in full by the original borrower upon sale or transfer of the property,

Balance Sheet: A financial statement that shows assets, liabilities and net worth as of a specific date.

Balloon Mortgage: A mortgage that has level monthly payments that will amortize it over a stated term but that provides for a lump sum payment to be due at the end

Balloon Payment: the final lump sum payment that is made at the maturity date of a balloon mortgage, of an earlier specified term.

Bankrupt: A person, firm, or corporation that, through a court proceeding, is relieved from the payment of ail debts after the surrender of all assets to a court-appointed trustee. Bankruptcy: A proceeding in a federal court In which a debtor who owes more than his or her assets can relieve the debts by transferring his or her assets to a trustee.

Before tax income: income before taxes are deducted.

Binder: A preliminary agreement secured by the payment of an earnest money deposit under which a buyer offers to purchase real estate.

Biweekly payment mortgage: a mortgage that requires payments to reduce the debt every two weeks (instead of the standard monthly payment schedule), The 26 (or possibly 27) biweekly payments are each equal to one-half of the monthly payment that would be required if the loan were a standard 30-year fixed-rate mortgage, and they are usually drafted from the borrower's bank account. The result for the borrower is a substantial savings in interest.

Blanket: Mortgage; the mortgage that is secured by a cooperative project as opposed to the share loans on individual units within the project,

Bond: An interest-bearing certificate of debt with a maturity date. An obligation of a government or business Corporation: real estate bond is a written obligation usually secured by a mortgage or a deed of trust.

Breach: a violation of any legal obligation,

Bridge loan: a form of second trust that is collateralized by the borrower's present home (which is usually for sate) in a manner that allows the proceeds to be used for closing on a new house before the present home is sold. Also known as "swing loan,"

Broker: a person who, for a commission or a fee, brings parties together and assists in negotiating contracts between them.

Buy Down Mortgage: a temporary buy down is a mortgage on which an initial lump sum payment is by any party to reduce a borrower's monthly payments during the first few years of a mortgage. A permanent buy reduces the interest rate over the entire life of a loan.

Call Option: a provision in the mortgage that gives the mortagagee the right to call the mortgage due and payable at the end of a specified period for whatever reason, Cap: A provision of an adjustable-rate (ARM) that limits how the interest rate or mortgage payments may increase or decrease

Capital Improvement: any structure or component erected as a permanent improvement to real Property that adds to its value and useful life,

Cash out: refinance A refinance transaction in which the amount of money received from the new (loan exceeds the total of the money needed to repay the existing first mortgage, dosing costs, points, and the amount required to satisfy any outstanding subordinate mortgage liens; In other words a refinanced transaction in which the borrower receives additional 'cash that can be used for any purpose.

Certificate of Eligibility: a document issued by the federal government certifying a veteran's eligibility for a Department of Veterans Affairs (VA) mortgage.

Certificate of Reasonable Value (CRV): A document issued by The Department of Veterans Affairs (VA) that establishes the maximum value and loan amount for a VA mortgage.

Certificate of title: a statement provided by an abstract company (tide company) or attorney stating the title to real estate is legally held by the current owner.

Chain of title: the history of alt of the documents that transfer title to a parcel of real property starting with the earliest existing document and ending with the most recent.

Change frequency: the frequency (in months) of payment and/or interest rate changes in an Adjustable-fate mortgage (ARM)

Clear title: a title that is free of Hens or legal questions as to ownership of the property.

Closing: a meeting at which a sale of a property is finalized by the buyer (s) signing the mortgage documents and paying closing costs. Also called "settlement."

Closing cost item: a fee or amount that a buyer must pay at closing for a single service, tax, or product. Closing costs are made up of Individual closing cost items such as origination fees and attorney's fees. Many closing cost items are included as numbered items on the HUD1 statement.

Closing costs: expenses (over and above the price of the property) incurred by buyers and sellers in transferring ownership of a property. Closing costs normally include an origination fee, an attorney's fee, taxes, an amount placed in escrow, and charges for obtaining title insurance and a survey. Closing costs percentage will vary according to the area of the country-

Closing statement also referred to as the HUD1. The final statement of costs incurred to close on a loan or to purchase a home.

Cloud on title: any conditions revealed by a title search that adversely affect the title to real estate. Usually clouds on title cannot be removed except by a quitclaim deed, release, or court action

Collateral: an asset (such as a car or a home) that guarantees the repayment of a loan. The borrower risks losing their assets if the loan is not repaid according to the terms of the loan contract.

Collection: The efforts used to bring a delinquent mortgage current and to file the necessary notices to proceed with foreclosure when necessary.

Co-maker: a person who signs a promissory note along with the borrower. A co-maker's signature guarantees that the loan will be repaid, because the borrower and the co-maker are equally responsible for the repayment. See endorser.

Commission: The fee charged by a broker or agent for negotiating a real estate or loan transaction. A commission is generally a percentage of the price of the properly or loan.

Commitment letter: a formal offer by a lender stating the terms under which it agrees to lend money to a homebuyer. Also known as a "loan commitment

Common areas: those portions of a building, land, and amenities owned (or managed) by a planned unit development (PUD) or condominium projects homeowners association (or a cooperative project's cooperative corporation) that are used by all of the unit owners, who share in the common expenses of their operation and maintenance. Common areas include swimming pools, tennis courts, and other recreational facilities, as well as common corridors

Community Home Improvement Mortgage Loan: An alternative financing option that allows low- and moderate-income home buyers to obtain 95 percent financing for the purchase and improvement of a home in need of modest repairs. The repair work can account for as much as 30 percent of the appraised value.

Community Property: Property owned equally by a husband and wife. This classification of property is only used in certain states.

Compatibles: An abbreviation for "comparable properties" used for comparative purposes in the appraisal process. Comparables are properties like the property under consideration; they have reasonably the same size, location and amenities and have recently been sold.

Comparables help the appraiser determine the approximate fair market value of the subject property.

Condominium: A real estate project in which each unit owner has title to a unit in a building, an undivided interest in the common areas of the project, and sometimes the exclusive use of certain limited common areas.

Condominium Conversion: changing the ownership of an existing building (usually a rental project) to the condominium form of ownership.

Construction Loan: a short-term, interim loan for financing the cost of construction. The lender makes payments to the builder at periodic intervals as the work progresses.

Consumer Reporting agency (or bureau): An organization that prepares reports used by lenders to determine a potential borrower's credit history. The agency obtains data for these reports from a credit repository as well as from other sources.

Contingency: a condition that must be met before a contract is legally binding. For example, home purchasers often include a contingency that specifies that the contract is not binding until the purchaser obtains a satisfactory home inspection report from a qualified home inspector.

Contract: an oral or written agreement to do or not to do a certain thing.

Conventional Mortgage: a mortgage that is not insured or guaranteed by the federal government.

Convertibility clause: a provision in some adjustable-rate mortgages (ARM) that allows the borrower to change the ARM to a fixed-rate mortgage at specified timeframes after loan origination.

Convertible ARM: an adjustable-rate mortgage (ARM) that can be converted to a fixed-rate mortgage under specified conditions.

Cooperative (co-op): A type of multiple ownership in which the residents of a multiunit housing complex own shares in the cooperative corporation that owns the property, giving each resident the right to occupy a specific apartment or unit.

Corporate Relocation: arrangements under which an employer moves an employee to another area as part of the employer's normal course of business or under which it transfers a substantial part or all of its operations and employees to another area because it is relocating its headquarters or expanding its office capacity.

Cost of funds index (COFI): An index that is used to determine interest rate changes for certain adjustable-rate mortgage (ARM) plans. It represents the weighted-average cost of savings, borrowings, and advances of the 11th District members of the Federal Home Loan Bank of San Francisco.

Covenant: A clause in a mortgage that obligates or restricts the borrower and that, if violated, can result in foreclosure.

Credit: An agreement in which a borrower receives something of value in exchange for a promise to repay the lender at a later date.

Credit History: a record of an individual's open and fully repaid debts. A credit history helps a lender to determine whether a potential borrower has a history of repaying debts in a timely manner.

Credit Report: A report of an individual's credit history prepared by a credit bureau and used by a lender in determining a loan applicant's creditworthiness. See merged credit report.

Credit Repository: an organization that gathers, records, updates, and stores financial and public records information about the payment records of individuals who are being considered for credit.

Debt: an amount owed to another.

Deed: the legal document conveying title to a property.

Deed-in-lieu: a deed given by a mortgagor to the mortgagee to satisfy a debt and avoid foreclosure.

Deed of trust: the document used in some states instead of a mortgage; title is conveyed to a trustee

Default: failure to make mortgage payments on a timely basis or to comply with other requirements of a mortgage Delinquent: failure to make mortgage payments when mortgage payments are due.

Deposit: A sum of money given to bind the sale of real estate, or a sum of money given to ensure payment or an advance of funds in the processing of a loan.

Depreciation: a decline in the value of property; the opposite of appreciation,

Due-on-sale provision: a provision in a mortgage that allows the lender to demand repayment in full if the borrower sells the property that serves as security for the mortgage.

Down Payment: The part of the purchase price of a property that the buyer pays in cash and does not finance with a mortgage.

Earnest Money Deposit: a deposit made by the potential home purchaser to show that he or she is serious about buying the house.

Escrow disbursements: the use of escrow funds to pay real estate taxes, hazard insurance, mortgage insurance, and other property expenses as they become due.

Escrow payment: the portion of a mortgagor's monthly payment that is held by the services to pay for taxes, hazard insurance, mortgage insurance, lease payments, and other items as they become due. Known as "impounds" or "reserves" in some states.

Estate: the ownership interest of an individual in real property. The sum total of all the real property and personal property owned by an Individual at time of death.

Eviction: the lawful expulsion of an occupant from real property.

Examination of title: the report on the title of a property from the public records or an abstract of the Title.

Fair Credit Reporting Act: a consumer protection law that regulates the disclosure of consumer credit reports by consumer/credit reporting agencies and establishes procedures for correcting mistakes on one's credit record.

Fair market value: The highest price that a buyer willing, but not compelled to buy or would pay and the lowest a seller is willing but not compelled to accept.

Fannie Mae: A congressionally chartered, shareholder-owned company that is the nation's largest supplier of home mortgage funds.

Fannie Mac's Community Home Buyer's Program: An income-based community lending model, under which mortgage insurers and Fannie Mae offer flexible underwriting guidelines to increase a low-or moderate-income family's buying power and to decrease the total amount of cash needed to purchase a home. Borrowers who participate in this model are required to attend pre-purchase homebuyer education sessions.

Federal Housing Administration (FHA): an agency of the U.S. Department of Housing and Urban Development (HUD) Its main activity is the insuring of residential mortgage loans made by private

Lenders. The FHA sets standards for construction and underwriting but does not tend money or plan or construct housing.

Fee simple: The greatest possible interest a person can have in real estate.

FHA mortgage: A mortgage that is insured by the Federal Housing Administration (FHA). Also known as a government mortgage.

FHA Loans: (Federal Housing Administration): FHA loans are available to help people who can't necessarily afford a 10% down payment on their new home. If approved, the Federal Housing Administration will cover up to 97.75% of the purchase price, thus bringing the down payment to a low 3-5%.

Please refer to Fannie Mae... Freddie Mac... HUD for update and accurate information periodically

Who Qualifies? Luckily, you don't have to have squeaky-dean credit to be approved. FHA approval is dependent on your overall debt-to-income ratio. If your debt-to-income ratio is below 41% there is a good chance you will qualify. However, if you live in a city where even first-time buyers are paying over $180,000 for a house, your chances of being approved are slim to none. Current Maximum

FHA Mortgage Limits:
Current Standard-cost limits: FHA (b) Floors One-family: $81,548 Two-family: $104,329 Three-family: $126,103 Four-family: $256,731 Current High-cost limits:

Finders fee: a fee or commission paid to a mortgage broker for finding a mortgage loan for a prospective borrower.

First mortgage: a mortgage that is the primary lien against a property.

Fixed-rate mortgage: (FRM): a mortgage in which the interest rate does not change during the entire term of the loan.

Flood insurance: Insurance that compensates for physical property damage resulting from flooding. It is required for properties located in federally designated flood areas

Foreclosure: The legal process by which a borrower in default under a mortgage is deprived of his or her interest in the mortgaged property. This usually involves a forced sate of the property at public auction with the proceeds of the sale being applied to the mortgage debt.

Fully amortized ARM: An adjustable-rate mortgage (ARM) with a monthly payment that is sufficient to amortize the remaining balance, at the interest accrual rate, over the amortization term.

Good faith Estimate: An estimate of charges in which a borrower is likely to incur in connection with a settlement.

Hazard Insurance: Insurance protecting against loss to real estate caused by fire, some natural causes, vandalism, etc., depending upon the terms of the policy.

Housing Ratio: the ratio of the monthly housing payment in total (PHI -Principal, Interest, Taxes, and Insurance) divided by the gross monthly income. This ratio is sometimes referred to as the top ratio or front-end ratio.
HUD: The U.S. Department of Housing and Urban Development

Index: A published interest rate to which the interest rate on an Adjustable Rate Mortgage (ARM) (s tied. Some commonly used indices include the 1 Year Treasury, 6 Month UBOR, and the 11th District Cost of Funds (COFI).

Installment debt: regular periodic payment that a borrower agrees to make to a lender. (Car loans, student loans, etc.) This does not include your mortgage payment.

Interest only loan option: Loan payments have two components, principal and interest. An interest-only loan has no principal component for a specified period of time. These special loans minimize your monthly payments by eliminating the need to pay down your balance during the interest-only period, giving you greater cash flow control and/or increased purchasing power.

Lien: an encumbrance against property for money due, either voluntary or involuntary.

Lifetime cap: A provision of an ARM that limits the highest rate that can occur over the life of the loan.

Loan to value ratio (LTV): ratio of the amount of your loan to the appraised value of the home. The LTV will affect programs available to the borrower and generally, the lower the LTV the more favorable the terms of the programs offered by lender set rate that can occur over the life of the loan.

Lock-in: A written agreement guaranteeing the homebuyer a specified interest rate provided the loan is closed within a set period of time. The lock-in also usually specifies the number of points to be paid at closing. Margin: The number of percentage points a lender adds to the index value to calculate the ARM interest rate at each adjustment period. A representative margin would be 2.75%.

Mortgage: A legal document that pledges a property to the lender as security for payment of a debt

Mortgage disability insurance: A disability insurance policy, which will pay the monthly mortgage payment in the event of a covered disability of an insured borrower for a specified period of time.

Mortgage insurance (MI): Insurance written by an independent mortgage insurance company protecting the mortgage and lender against loss Incurred by a mortgage default. Usually required for loans with an LTV of 80.01% or higher.

Mortgagee: the person or company who receives the mortgage as a pledge for repayment of the loan. The mortgage lender

Mortgagor: the mortgage borrower who gives the mortgage as a pledge to repay.

Non-conforming loan: Also called a jumbo loan. Conventional home mortgages not eligible for sale and delivery to either Fannie Mae (FNMA) or Freddie Mac (FHLMC) because of various reasons, including loan amount, loan characteristics or underwriting guidelines. Non-conforming loans usually incur a rate and origination fee premium. The current non-conforming loan limit is $333,701 and above.

No documentation loans: A no-documentation or "no-doc" mortgage is a product that certain lenders offer to borrowers which generally requires a down payment of at least 5% to 30% or more of the home purchase price or who generally have at least 25% equity in their home. Loan programs featuring lower down payments (5-24%) are also available to borrowers with excellent credit.

No-doc mortgages are generally a wise choice for self-employed people, those who do not wish to verify their income, and those with a brief or blemished credit history, or no credit "The benefits of a no-doc mortgage include a shorter application process since you are not required to provide income, employment or asset documentation, as well as a streamlined approval process through the lender because there is little subsequent verification. However, no doc mortgages generally will be at slightly higher interest rates and are offered by fewer lenders.

Note: A written agreement containing a promise of the signer to pay to a named person, or order, or bearer, a definite sum of money at a specified date or on demand.

Origination fee: A fee imposed by a lender to cover certain processing expenses in connection with making a real estate loan. Usually a percentage of the amount loaned, such as one percent.

Owner financing: A property purchase transaction in which the property seller provides all or part of the financing. Planned Unit Developments (PUD) A subdivision of five or more individually owned lots with one or more other parcels owned in common or with reciprocal rights in one or more other parcels.

PITI- Principal, interest, taxes and insurance: the components of a monthly mortgage payment

Points: Charges levied by the mortgage lender and usually payable at closing. One point represents 1% of the face value of the mortgage loan.

Prepaid: Those expenses of property which are paid in advance of their due date and will usually be prorated upon sale, such as taxes, insurance, rent, etc.

Prepayment penalty: A charge imposed by a mortgage lender on a borrower who wants to pay off part or all of a mortgage loan in advance of schedule.

Principal: Amount of debt not including interest. The face value of a note or mortgage.

Private mortgage insurance (PHX): Insurance provided by nongovernmental insurers that protect lenders against loss if a borrower defaults. Fannie Mae generally requires private mortgage insurance for loans with loan-to-value (LTV) percentages greater than 80%.

Qualifying ratios: The ratio of your fixed monthly expenses to your gross monthly income, used to determine how much you could afford to borrow. The fixed monthly expenses would include Pm along with other obligations such as student loans, car loans, or credit card payments

Rate cap: A limit on how much the Interest rate can change, either at each adjustment period or over the life of the loan.

Rate lock-in: A written agreement, in which the lender guarantees the borrower a specified interest rate, provided the loan closes within a set period of time.

Rebate: Compensation received from a wholesale lender, which can be used to cover closing costs, or as a refund to the borrower. Loans with rebates often carry higher interest rates than loans with "points" (see above).

Refinancing: the process of paying off one loan with the proceeds from a new loan using the same property as security.

Residential mortgage credit report (RMCR) A report requested by your lender that utilizes information from at least two of the three national credit bureaus and information provided on your loan application.

Revolving debt: A credit arrangement, such as a credit card, that allows a customer to borrow against a pre-approved line of credit when purchasing goods and services. The borrower is billed for the amount that is actually borrowed plus any interest due, (i.e. your Visa, Master Card, American Express, Discover cards + all of your department store credit cards.)

Seller carry back: An agreement in which the owner of a property provides financing, often in combination with an assumed mortgage.

Stated/documented income: Some loan products require only that applicants "state" the source of their income without providing supporting documentation such as tax returns.

Survey: A print showing the measurements of the boundaries of a parcel of land, together with the location of alt improvements on the land and sometimes its area and topography.

Tenants-in-common: an undivided interest in property taken by two or more persons. The interest need not be equal. Upon death of one or more persons, there is no right of survivorship

Title: The evidence one has of right to possession of land

Title insurance: Insurance against loss resulting from defects of title to a specifically described parcel of real property,

Title search: An investigation into the history of ownership of a property to check for liens, unpaid claims, restrictions or problems, to prove that the seller can transfer free and clear ownership.

Total debt ratio: Monthly debt and housing payments divided by gross monthly income. Also known as Obligations-to-income Ratio or Back-End Ratio.

Truth-in-Lending Act: A federal law requiring a disclosure of credit terms using a standard format this is intended to facilitate comparisons between the lending terms of different financial institutions.

Veterans Administration (VA): A government agency guaranteeing mortgage loans with no down payment to qualified veterans.

VA loans (Veteran Affairs): Millions of military veterans and service personnel are eligible for VA financing each year. Even if you have already used VA loan benefits in the past, you may be able to use remaining or restored loan entitlement to buy another home. This is an excellent service benefit because it requires zero down payments in most cases. VA buyers may also have all of their closing costs paid by the seller. Loans generally may not exceed $203,000. Who Qualifies?

- Veterans and service personnel with active duty service, that was not dishonorable.

Made in the USA
San Bernardino, CA
19 January 2017